Travels While On My Journey

Ed Hearn

Travels While On My Journey

Major Trips From My Life

LEGACY IV BOOKS

Published by Legacy IV Books

ehearn@ec.rr.com

Published 2018 – First Edition

Copyright © 2018 by Ed Hearn

ISBN 978-1-71941-483-8

Printed in the United States of America

Set in Times New Roman

Editing and proofreading by Trent Armbruster

Cover Design and Concept by Sara Morris

Interior Design by Abigail Chiaramonte

*This book is
dedicated to
Trent Armbruster*

*She made each of these
exciting trips possible
for me*

Preface

I would like to thank Trent Armbruster for the time, money and effort she put into each of the trips that I list in this book, *Travels while on my Journey...Major Trips from my Life.* She has served as an excellent personal travel agent, close friend, and life partner while scheduling the airlines, rental cars, lodging locations, and working out all the details for additional side trips along the way. Without her participation, none of these travels would have happened.

She has been extremely flexible so that changes could be made at the last minute to maximize the overall experience. I've had to do very little organizing of the itineraries and bookings. Some of the times, I didn't even know what was about to happen until boarding the plane in Wilmington, North Carolina when she would hand me an itinerary or travel book about where we were going that day. That has worked perfectly because I don't like to deal with the details, or wait for a particular trip to occur after it has been set up.

Sometimes we have gone on these trips together, and sometimes I have gone by myself. Either way, I always knew that everything had been worked out in advance, and that all I had to do was follow her instructions.

I have traveled all over the world in the past twenty years and experienced some amazing sights and people. Some of the places I have been include Alaska, Puerto Rico, Dominican Republic, Bermuda, Cayman Islands, Bahamas, Turks and Caicos, St. Thomas, St. John, St. Croix, Virgin Gorda, Antigua, Barbados, St. Lucia, St. Martin, St. Kitts, Nevis, Aruba, Curacao, Bonaire, Belize, Guatemala, all four of the major islands in Hawaii, both islands in New Zealand, Australia, Argentina, Brazil, Spain, France, Italy, Africa, China, South Korea, Canada, Mexico, Costa Rica and almost every state in the continental United States.

After each trip was completed and I arrived back home, I usually became aware I was no longer the same person as when I had left. I realized my exposure to the different countries, cultures, and its varied people always altered who I was, and the way I viewed the world. I think that's the way all travel should be, a learning experience that causes us to change and evolve in our thinking. It definitely causes us to form new viewpoints toward our surroundings and who we are as individuals.

During only ten of those exciting trips did I take the time to keep a daily journal documenting my adventures. I wish now I had done it more frequently to help retain more of those memories for the future. In this book, you will find all ten of those for your enjoyment. Some of the trips were so I could compete in World Masters Track and Field Championships in Brazil, Australia and South Korea. Other trips were to hunt, fish, and search for ancient dinosaur fossils, or just to explore unusual places.

On each outing there was always lots of excitement, and on a few, there was some danger. As I look back over the past twenty years, since I retired and started traveling, I've certainly been fortunate to have been able to tour the world. It was something I never thought I would be able to do in my lifetime.

I hope you enjoy the stories included in this book about major trips from my life. On one trip in particular, I didn't think I would be coming back alive.

Contents

Belize, Central America
January 2003

Trent and I both enjoy traveling. In January of 2003, we decided to visit Belize, Central America.

Before we left home, I talked to my brother, Jim, who had just returned from an exciting trip to Costa Rica, which is located south of Belize. For him, going there had been nonstop fun, and he described all of the eco-adventures and side trips he had taken. I thought Belize would have similar opportunities for Trent and me.

I got excited, but really didn't know what to expect on our upcoming trip. Jim mentioned he was still taking malaria tablets, because he had been in a jungle setting and exposed to mosquitos possibly infected with the malaria virus. That made me think, for the first time, I needed to check with a doctor and get the necessary shots and prescriptions before going to that unfamiliar place in Central America.

An appointment was made with a doctor in Wilmington who specialized in treating people who traveled to exotic places. He was familiar with diseases not common in the United States. After he gave me a few injections of vaccine, he wrote me prescriptions for a variety of pills. It was a surprise to me I needed that attention, because I almost went on the trip without making any advance medical preparations.

During the doctor's visit, I felt like a pin cushion while receiving a tetanus shot, a hepatitis shot and a yellow fever shot. He suggested I consider getting a new polio shot, but later decided, based on where we were going, it wasn't totally necessary. Because of that conversation, I passed on it.

Trent decided to visit the same doctor and get the treatment I had just gone through. We were both given prescriptions for malaria tablets to start taking immediately, and were to continue taking those for three to four weeks after we got back home. He also gave us an antibiotic to combat diarrhea, in case we ate something bad or drank water that contained the E. coli bacteria, which was fairly common in that part of the world.

After packing enough gear to last for fifteen days, we left for the airport in Wilmington on January 16th. The trip began by flying west to Charlotte. After an hour layover, we boarded a jet that flew us directly to Belize. That flight took three and a half hours. It dropped us directly into a whole different environment.

Our first destination was Belize City on the Caribbean side of the country, located directly on the eastern coast. That seemed to be a good starting place. The country is five hundred miles from north to south and two hundred miles from east to west. It is bordered on the north by Mexico and on the south and west by Guatemala. My understanding before traveling there was that it contained many diverse ecosystems. I later found that to be true.

Belize City was a small area with about 70,000 people. Most of them seemed friendly and spoke good English. I learned Belize is the only country in Central America with English as its native language, having once been owned by the British.

While in Belize City for the first few days, we stayed in the Radisson Hotel directly on the coast, where the lodging was first class, and the food was very good. We drank the water there with no fear of getting sick. From our large picture window in the hotel, we overlooked the bay where there were dive ships, cruise ships and old sailing ships with large sails and masts docked along the shoreline. There were many handmade, colorful boats docked there, which the locals used to fish and take tourists from one location to the other. I noticed unusual birds flying in the air and landing in the trees around us. That was of interest to me because of all the bird sculpture carving I had done.

My first shopping trip in Belize City was to go to a book store and purchase the best book I could find showing color pictures of the birds in the Central American region. I wanted to be able to identify and learn the names of the birds I saw as we traveled across the country. As the days went by, I began to mark in the book every time we spotted a different bird and where it had been sighted. When the trip ended, I was hoping to be surprised at how many species I had been able to observe.

During our stay in Belize City, we scheduled a few day tours to outlying areas of interest. The first day we employed a guide, named Roy, who had his own car. He drove us on an all-day trip to two different attractions. The first location was the Crooked Tree Wildlife Reserve. It had obtained its name from a very unusual tree that stood in the middle of the area and was shaped like a giant cork screw. The second location was a large Mayan ruin named Altun Ha.

Upon arriving at the reserve, we drove the car to a small home near the front of the property. We were greeted by a smiling family and a dark skinned man who was to take us on a boat ride around a large, calm lake. The reserve was a combination of woods, jungle and a lake that ran through it. I was mostly interested in the bird life that lived along the shores and in the trees surrounding the lake. The sky was overcast that day, so our outing ended up being very comfortable as we spotted numer-ous species of birds. Those included hawks, eagles, herons and smaller, colorful birds I had never seen before. We cruised along the shoreline at a moderate speed and slowed when something interesting was spotted.

The trip was highlighted by sighting a rare, black collared hawk in a marshy area near the back side of the lake. Its head and face were cream-colored with a black ring around its neck, while the body was a beautiful rust color with black primary wing tips. There were other sightings that first day including the common black hawk, tiger heron, vermillion flycatcher, ringed kingfisher and pygmy kingfisher. Our three hour boat trip ended with a meal cooked by a local family and served in a thatched hut with a screened porch. We ate cooked chicken and rice, but avoided the fruit tea because of a fear of drinking the local water in that remote place. Everything worked out fine, and we didn't get sick.

After leaving Crooked Tree Wildlife Reserve, we traveled down a very bumpy, washed out, dirt road for many miles to arrive at Altun Ha, the Mayan ruin. It had been discovered in the middle of the jungle during the early 1950s and was totally overgrown with vegetation. We were told the Mayan people had occupied that spot from 200 B.C. until around 800 A.D. For some unknown reason, they had abandoned all the temples spread across the Central American area somewhere between 800 A.D. and 1000 A.D.

The area was supposed to have been a large trading center for the Mayas who lived from Mexico to Guatemala to Honduras. It was hard to believe that the ancient people could have traveled those distances through the dense jungle to trade wares from such faraway places. Some of the items traded included green jade used for carving jewelry and different types of pottery.

We noticed very little had been done to the ancient temples, made of large stones, since they were first discovered. Some of the mounds were still covered with jungle growth and dirt. Slowly, a few of the larger ones were being uncovered. A group of men were busy doing that on the day we visited. The temples looked a little like the photos I had seen of the pyramids in Egypt, though not nearly as big. There were many similarities. I took a lot of good photos as we observed that unusual place.

The next day we set two goals. We wanted to visit another large nature reserve and then see the local zoo. Our plans were to rent a car to travel south instead of north, as we had done the day before. Most of the roads had no pavement and were in bad condition. They were filled with pot holes. This trip had us driving onto a main road that went west across the country from Belize City for about a hundred miles, called the Western Highway, and then south onto Hummingbird Highway. Fortunately, both of those main highways in the central part of the country were paved.

One of the things we found out pretty fast was that the Belizean people were not too concerned about making or putting up road signs. Over the first week, and on that day, we got lost many times. On one occasion, we traveled as far as twenty miles down a bumpy, dirt road looking for a sign. We asked someone walking along the side of the road where we had gone wrong and had to backtrack, since we had missed our turnoff.

We made our scheduled stops at the Baboon Wildlife Reserve and the Belize Zoo. The Baboon Wildlife Reserve's name was a little misleading, because the local people referred to the black howler monkeys that lived there in the trees as baboons. There are only two species of monkeys that live in Belize. One is the black howler monkey and the other is the spider monkey. The black howler monkey is the only one left in the wild, and the spider monkey is now only found in special zoos. The spider monkey had been mainly killed off a few years earlier by the smallpox virus, and the remaining few survive in captivity.

Another interesting fact was that the reserve was actually just a collection of small farms where the owners charged the tourists to come onto their land and see the monkeys in the trees. The first farm had a big sign indicating it was the main office for the reserve. There, we were greeted by a small family of friendly people speaking very good English. We were asked if we were interested in seeing the black howler monkeys. After paying five dollars each for the opportunity, a guide took us into the woods.

The guide told us the monkeys lived in small groups of five to eight, and the groups were separated by as much as a mile throughout the woods. We walked through dense trees and a jungle setting while everyone looked up, searching the trees. It wasn't long before two were sighted twenty feet up in a large tree. They were totally black, full of short hair, and looked like I would have expected, with long tails to help them maneuver through the dense trees. They were two to three feet tall. As we walked under them, the guide explained the monkeys got their name by the loud noise they made when excited or when they called their mate.

Since they were all being very quiet, I took some close-up photos with my telephoto lens. Then the guide decided it was time to let us hear the sound the monkeys made when irritated. He began to make growling noises and grunting sounds. Before long, the monkeys let out extremely loud screams that almost made me jump out of my shirt. They sounded as if they were really mad and were about to leap out of the trees on top of us. For little monkeys, it was surprising how loud and scary they could be. We were told the screams could be heard a mile away.

I got some good photos and decided it was time to leave the woods because the mosquitos were beginning to bite. As the trees opened up into a large field, just a few hundred yards from the road where the car was parked, we saw a whole flock of dark green parakeets flying overhead. They were twelve inches long from their heads to the end of their tails, and they landed in some nearby trees. With my binoculars, I was able to get a really good look at them. I knew the overall species of "parakeets" included those green birds a foot in length or less. A similar species called "parrots" are those larger colorful green birds. We saw both in the wild during our trip that day.

Our next stop was to the Belize Zoo located an hour's drive from the Baboon Wildlife Reserve. Again, it didn't look like much from the main road, and if we had blinked our eyes, we would have missed it. We pulled the car in, parked, and paid our entrance fee at the main office. In the woods around the zoo, but not in any type of caged area, we spotted orioles in yellow and black colors and tanagers with beautiful, solid red feathers. I got a few pictures of them before they flew away into the woods.

Inside the zoo, we were able to see many unusual birds and animals of Belize. There were different kinds of cats, including ocelots and panthers, plus hawks, macaw parrots and spider monkeys, to name a few. Most of the wildlife was contained in large pens that included natural settings. In some cases, those enclosures made it hard to see the animals and birds through the wire cages and trees, especially if they were hiding or asleep.

We later left the zoo with a better understanding of some of the rarer animals and birds seldom seen by tourists in the wild. Overall, it was an interesting stop, and I was really glad we made it. What a special treat it was!

On January 19th, we traveled from Belize City along that same route south to the little town of Plancencia on the eastern coast of the Caribbean. Naturally, we got lost and traveled ten miles too far south before deciding we had missed our turn. After backtracking, we found a little dirt country road that was indicated on the map as the only way to Plancencia, where we were to stay for a few days. We found it to be the bumpiest dirt road we had ever been on.

As we made that long, slow trip, we stopped occasionally, and I did some birding with my binoculars. The whole trip south, including getting lost, took us six hours. As you can imagine, by the time we finally arrived, we were both exhausted. We stayed at a place named The Inn at Roberts Grove, where we had reservations. It was first class and a very nice, isolated resort with a five star restaurant. The place had been built by a couple from the United States who went there many years earlier on vacation, and decided to buy some land on the coast to build a house. Before long they decided to expand their home into a small resort and manage it personally year round. We talked with the owners during our stay, and they were both very nice.

The day after arriving in Plancencia, we decided to go on an outing listed on the Belize map, to a place named the Monkey River Reserve. We drove the rental car, with its bad air conditioner, an hour to that spot. A guide was available, who took us on a boat ride into the deep jungle and down the Monkey River.

Off we went through mangrove clusters and past many small islands on the way through the reserve.

Our guide explained that the main jungle had been destroyed a few years earlier by a hurricane. Where there had been huge canopy trees and large stands of bamboo, it now looked like loggers had come in and cut down almost everything. That storm had been very bad for the jungle, but already small trees had begun to grow in the open areas. We were told it would take those small trees seventy-five to one hundred years to grow back to the same height as before the storm.

The guide then took us to a little village up the river where he lived. There were maybe thirty people who lived there in four different one-room houses. Everyone appeared to be happy. They were smiling and waving as we arrived.

When we got out of the boat for a bathroom break, the village people pointed out a group of black howler monkeys and some iguanas climbing in the trees close by. We had already seen the howler monkeys, but it was a treat to see the large iguanas lying on limbs high in the trees. Some were three to four feet in length and bright orange in color. We were told those were the males and that the females were usually smaller and dark green. It was surprising how high some of the large males had climbed, and they looked like small alligators lying on the larger limbs in the dense trees some thirty to forty feet from the ground.

We noticed a small cage that contained two green parakeets located under one of the raised one-room houses. Those were not like the ones normally seen in pet stores, but much larger and broader. One was a red-lore parakeet, and the other was a yellow-headed parakeet. Both were very pretty. We were told they had been trapped in the jungle nearby.

The Monkey River Reserve trip included seeing many more unusual birds, more howler monkeys and exactly what a hurricane could do to destroy a jungle. We got out of the boat at a spot near the jungle's edge and walked down a very slick mud path for a quarter of a mile. The guide explained that we should be careful because there were poisonous snakes in the jungle and many trees full of thorns near the path's edge.

We came to some rotted trees that had fallen over the mud path, and the guide pointed out a large group of black ants moving across the ground in a long line. They were a little scary, because I wasn't sure how aggressively they would bite if they got on my skin. As I tried to step over a heavy line of them, my tennis shoes slipped in the mud, and down I went. I caught my binoculars, my camera and backpack, just before landing in the mud beside them by extending my arm into the underbrush. I was up and out of there quickly.

The guide continued to talk about the damage done to the jungle by the hurricane, and then got into a story about the time he had been attacked by a wild pig on that exact trail. He told us the aggressive pig had large curved tusks on either side of its mouth and had attacked him over and over. He had been with a group of tourists, and every time one of the tourists had tried to get the pig off him, it would attack that person also. The animal ripped into his arms with the large curved tusks, and the guide ended up breaking his leg. Finally, some other guides came along and shot the wild pig with a shotgun. That horror story kept me on the alert for the rest of our trip through the jungle.

The pig story reminded me of another story an earlier guide had told us when he had been bitten by a deadly, poisonous coral snake over at the Crooked Tree Wildlife Reserve. He had been leading a group of tourists through the jungle beside a lake and stepped on a small red, black and yellow-banded coral snake about fifteen inches long. It bit him on the ankle. I knew from previous study that the venom from that snake would attack the human nervous system and could cause death within hours.

He explained the people of Belize used many of the plants in the jungle to treat illnesses. He had slowed down the deadly venom going through his body by chewing on the bark from one of those special plants. By chewing the bark, he explained, he had given himself an extra six hours before the venom spread throughout his system.

The guide told us he never let the tourists know he had been bitten. He continued to guide them for the next few hours. After finishing the tour, he calmly drove himself to the hospital in Belize City three hours away. By the time he arrived, he was already getting patches of dark red spots all over his body where the poison was affecting his blood circulation. He stayed in the hospital six days, and with their anti-venom treatments, he survived. He showed me what that plant looked like, and after finding some in the jungle, I peeled off the bark and started carrying it in my pocket.

The day after the Monkey River Reserve trip, we looked on the map and found another interesting place to visit a few hours away. The toughest part was that we had to travel on that same bumpy, dirt road that ran parallel to the coast to get anywhere. Later in the day, we would have to go back down the same road to get home for the night. In spite of all that, we chose to drive to the Cockscomb Jaguar Wildlife Reserve one hundred miles inland.

That reserve reminded me of a big national forest, but it was actually a jungle area near the foothills of the western mountains. Upon arriving, and while climbing out of the car, I immediately sighted a passerini's tanager near the check-in station. That bird was about the size of a robin, but solid black except for a large patch on its back that was vivid red. The contrast of color was incredible to see as the bird flew from tree to tree.

While checking in and paying our fee to visit the reserve, I looked outside and noticed two small gray foxes near the thick underbrush within fifty feet of the building. With my telephoto lens already mounted on my camera, I was able to take some good pictures of them. Later, we sighted one of them traveling down the path that led back into the jungle. When we approached, it quickly moved into the underbrush until we passed.

We looked over the reserve map and decided to take one of the paths that was estimated to take an hour and a half to walk from start to finish. I knew it would take a little longer because I was planning to stop along the way and take some pictures. In fact, it took an hour longer.

As we entered the canopied jungle, one of the first things I noticed was how large the palms and vegetation grew under the tall trees. It was like being in the movie *Jurassic Park*. Everything was over-sized. Hidden throughout the undergrowth were beautiful flowering plants in bright shades of yellow and red. Some were versions of the interesting bird-of-paradise plant with its brightly colored flowers. We saw many different sizes and shapes. Up in the trees there were orchids attached to the trunks and limbs, with numerous vines growing up the sides of the trees while hanging down forty or fifty feet to the jungle floor.

Many small birds were flying through the trees as we walked. After each sighting, I would look in my bird book and identify what I had just seen. It seemed as if each bird was different from anything we had previously spotted. Very seldom did we see the same thing twice.

We crossed a small stream using a man-made wooden bridge. Each time we crossed the water, I looked for tracks of the jaguars that lived throughout the jungle. Before I left the visitor's building, I had checked with the guard, and he told me the jaguars were nocturnal animals. They were not usually seen unless a person was going through the jungle early in the morning or late in the evening. We were also told that most of the time they would shy away from the tourists and our safety wasn't much of a concern. However, that particular danger was still on my mind as we traveled along the path.

We spotted our first trogon bird, which was very colorful and fourteen inches long. Vivid blues and yellows, along with other colors, marked the bird and made it one I had wanted to see. Later on our walk, we got to see the national bird of Belize, a keel-billed toucan. The bird was considered very rare, and we spotted a pair of them in a tree fifty feet away. After we got a fast look through the binoculars, the toucans were on their way deep into the jungle, but not before flying directly over us about fifteen feet above. The toucan was mostly black with a white patch on top of its upper rump, a bright red patch underneath and a bright yellow breast and face. Its bill was very long, curved downwards and contained shades of yellow, green, orange, blue and red. The toucan was another bird I had definitely hoped to see on our trip, and it was beautiful.

Continuing on our walk through the jungle, we came upon a beautiful butterfly. With its wings open, it stood out from everything else in the dark undergrowth. With the wings closed, it blended in with everything, since it was so dark on its underside a person could be looking directly at it and never notice it. With the wings opened, the whole surface was the brightest, royal blue color I had ever seen. It glistened in the sunlight. Shortly, after it had been only a few feet in front of us, it was gone into the jungle.

After two more hours on that nature walk, we decided to go back to our resort before it got too dark. Before we left, we noticed a sign indicating there was a downed plane that had crashed one tenth of a mile off the main road. Even though it was getting dark, I couldn't pass up the opportunity to see it. It didn't take long to find the aircraft in a mangled mess on the jungle floor. Later, we found out it had belonged to one of the researchers who flew in and out of the jungle in the early 1980s and had crashed through the trees. The pilot had somehow made it out alive, but as small as the plane was, it was hard to believe he had survived.

The next day, it was time to leave the coast and drive west clear across the country and into the mountains to Blancaneaux Lodge. We were told the drive up to the mountains would take four hours, but after getting seriously lost twice, the trip took a full eight hours. We stopped along the way to do some bird watching, as I continued to see new and unusual birds in the trees. The roads were terrible once we got off the main highway. We had to proceed slowly around the winding steep roads.

We passed a sign along the way indicating there was a butterfly farm just up a hill, and we decided to check it out. That stop added an hour to our trip, but we got to see exotic butterflies that had been raised from eggs collected in the jungle. The eggs had gone from hatched caterpillars, to the cocoon formed around them, to the final butterflies of all different colors. The farm made its money by shipping the cocoons to different places, such as museums and nature parks, mainly in the United States. It was another interesting place, and I was glad we took the time to see it.

Blancaneaux Lodge belonged to Francis Ford Coppola, the movie producer and screen writer from California. We were told he visited every few months as a way to get away from his business life, but that he was not there while we were. He had his own airstrip in the jungle just to the side of the lodge, so he could fly in and out and not have to deal with the bad roads.

The accommodations consisted of fourteen amazing, independent thatched huts. The roofs were made with palm leaves from the jungle. The walls were made from large bamboo shafts. Some of the rooms and decks were screened, but the main living areas were open to the jungle.

Each evening we had a friendly bat that would fly right over our heads and circle the room before finding its home in-between some of the bamboo shafts on the internal wall. The bath was tiled with large green ceramic tiles from Mexico. The shower had an opening to the outdoors, so birds could fly in and out if they wished. I found that very unusual, but nice. There was no television or phone in the room. The complex was located on a hillside next to a mountain stream with large waterfalls just to the front of our room. Each night we fell asleep to the sounds of the cascading water.

The lodge had a wonderful restaurant where we ate most of our meals. We were able to drink the water that came from the mountain stream after it was purified. The lodge had its own organic garden where they raised all the vegetables served in the restaurant. The salads were the best I had ever tasted. Each morning at daybreak there would be three men working in the garden picking the vegetables to be used for that day. There were orange trees directly beside the hut we stayed in, and each day I picked some of the oranges to eat during the afternoon. I've never tasted any that were fresher or juicier than those.

There was also a horse stable containing eighteen horses. We were told four of them were used by the staff for racing purposes in the closest town, and the others were used to take the visitors on daily horseback rides through the hillsides. Trent later got to ride Cocoa, and I got to ride Lightning. We had a fun two hour horseback ride to one of the waterfalls two miles away.

I got up early each morning and just walked around outdoors, close to where we were staying, to watch the birds as they moved through the trees.

On one of our days there, we decided to walk a nature trail on a hillside leading to a group of very large waterfalls. We thought it would take an hour and fifteen minutes, but took us much longer. The trail went up and down steep inclines, and we were both exhausted by the time we had only walked two miles. I knew the waterfalls couldn't have been much farther, but we turned to go back. As I was leading us along the path, my guess of where to step at one spot was totally wrong. I put my foot down and quickly sank up to my knees in mud. Black, thick mud covered both of my lower legs. I almost couldn't pull my tennis shoes out. It was a mess. I had to later get in the mountain stream to wash the mud from my legs and shoes.

On another day, we decided to take a day trip to a very large

Mayan ruin approximately two miles from the Guatemalan border in the high mountains of western Belize. That place promised to be more fabulous than Altun Ha, which we had visited
earlier. The name of this ruin was Xunantunich and pronounced
shoe-non-too-neck. It contained a number of stone temples, and
the largest temple was supposed to be one of the tallest buildings
in Belize. On our way to that ancient city, deep in the jungle, we
passed a stone quarry where there were machines taking large,
cream-colored boulders out of the earth. We couldn't figure out
what was going on, but later found out the stones were being
used at Xunantunich to replace large stones in the temple that
had deteriorated over the last two thousand years.

After parking our car, we approached the area of the temples.

The ruin was located down a long dirt road in the deep jungle
and was only accessible by taking the car across a small river.
Getting across the river was an experience in itself. The only
way to do that was to load our car onto an antique, flat ferry
which held two cars. The ferry was then pulled across the stream
using a human hand crank with a cable connected to trees on
each bank. There was a nice Belizean man who ran the ferry
and turned the crank for the trip across and the trip back later in
the evening. For those who didn't have a car or had arrived by
bus, there was a mile walk around the river to another crossing
location.

After parking our car, we approached the area of the temples.
I quickly noticed there was a large mound on the edge of a rise
that had not yet been uncovered. It was still grown over with
trees and vegetation. Walking around that mound, we entered
a large, flat courtyard covered with green grass and completely
surrounded with large temples on all four sides. The area looked
a little like a large football stadium with bleachers on all sides.
The temples had many long steps leading up to the top. Where
the stones had recently been cleaned and repaired, they were all
cream in color and very impressive. Those were my thoughts
as we first entered the ancient temple complex. I took a lot of

photos, but there was no way the photos would show how impressive the temples actually were.

Climbing up the large steps leading to the top made me think about the smaller Mayan people. Why had they made the steps so tall and hard to climb? Each step was maybe a foot tall and by the time we reached the top, my thigh muscles were burning. On that particular temple, there were nice, large carvings three-fourths of the way to the top that had originally wrapped around the entire structure and could be seen from miles above the treetops. The strip of symbols and carvings were probably twenty-five feet tall. Over the years, some of the stones had broken off and rolled down the hill, but what was left was very interesting.

We reached the top and looked out over the countryside. It took my breath away as I walked over to the edge, and my knees got weak just looking down. Standing at the top convinced me we were much higher than 130 feet, the estimated height of the largest temple. While standing there and looking out over the surrounding trees in the forest canopy, we looked across miles of rolling hills below and noticed we were higher than the vultures sailing above the treetops. I guess that was why they say the Mayan priests felt they were closer to their gods while standing at that elevation.

After viewing the entire area, we entered a small modern museum and learned more about the Mayans and the location. We were told it was originally settled in 200 to 400 B.C. and left idle by approximately 1000 A.D. That was similar to the same dates we had been given at the first Mayan ruin, Altun Ha, we had visited. The researchers could not decide exactly why the Mayans had left all the scattered temples, such as the ones in that complex that spread throughout Central America, within a hundred years of the same time. For the Mayans, that time was actually well before the Spanish explorers first arrived in Central America, so it was not believed the Spanish brought diseases or killed the Mayans. It was common knowledge that the Spanish did plunder the ruins and took many artifacts, including some made of gold and jade, when they arrived hundreds of years later.

As we boarded the hand-drawn ferry and crossed the stream back to the other side, we decided we were so close to the Guatemalan border we might as well cross and see what that country was like. We parked the car at the border, because we were not allowed to take the rental car across into another country. We were approached immediately by men who wanted to exchange our money for a fee.

Going through customs, showing our passports, and paying the entry fees, was standard procedure. We then caught a small cab and were taken into the nearest town where there was an open-air marketplace. I was very curious to see how different that place was from what we had been encountering throughout Belize. We were soon to find out it was very different.

The market area was not what we had expected. I had envisioned a tourist trap, but it was a real market for the local residents. Under blue tarp tents positioned very close together, the merchants had laid out on tables many different items for purchase. Those included assorted clothes, shoes, school bags for the children, food, fruit and everything we could imagine that would be used in daily life. It was not exactly like walking into our modern shopping malls, but it accomplished the same thing for those people.

What we were looking for in that market were the normal tourist shops, so we could buy some souvenirs, but we only found one place that fit that purpose. It contained many colorful fabrics, furniture coverings, baskets, weavings, pottery, slate carvings and carvings made from local woods. We didn't purchase anything there because all the colors looked too Mexican for us. The objects were pretty and painted in bright, strong colors with Mexican-like patterns, but we had no use for them back home.

The people of Guatemala were not as friendly or as helpful as those in Belize. They also did not speak English as easily as their nearby neighbors. We felt uncomfortable. As a result, we crossed the border after only two hours of walking around and immediately felt better about being back in Belize. We were glad we had made the short trip into Guatemala, so as to get a small taste of that country.

The next day, we left the mountains and traveled east across the country back to Belize City. We needed to return the rental car and board a boat to travel to our next destination. As we drove down a bumpy road surrounded by tall trees, I finally spotted one of the large and unusual birds I had been looking for throughout the trip. Right at the edge of the road, staring down at me, was a blue-crowned motmot. It was a large bird, fifteen inches tall, with a mixture of beautiful colors and a very unusual group of tail feathers. The tail feathers were longer than normal, but the last three inches narrowed to only the shaft on each feather for about two inches in length. The feathers then became regular and full again all the way to the end.

We passed large banana farms, orange orchards and fields of lime trees on our trip back to the ocean. We figured those farms must be part of a large industry managed by the government. There were numerous tenant houses lined up beside the mile long rows of banana plants and orange trees.

I spotted a laughing falcon sitting on the top of an electrical pole near the banana plants. The bird appeared to be a small hawk, but its coloring was unusual. The top of its head was white with a bold dark band across its face. The chest was cream-colored, with a dark back and barred tail feathers. As it flew from its perch, the movement was obviously not that of a normal hawk. Its shorter wings were more pointed and tucked, as the bird swooped low to the ground. It then shot upward to land on the top of another electrical pole a few hundred yards away. Its speed was impressive, and the bird showed no wasted motion as it moved from one location to the other.

Our next destination was to the village of San Pedro located on Ambergris Caye. That small island was 35 miles from the mainland. Downtown, in Belize City, we boarded what looked like a very old cigar boat used in the television series *Miami Vice*. To get to the island, we had to cross a large body of ocean water through rough waves. I didn't think there would be many people making the two hour trip to San Pedro with us, but I was wrong. Our luggage was loaded in the middle of the boat in a big pile, along with the luggage of at least sixty other people. Everyone on board sat on benches around the outer edges.

As I looked around the interior of the boat, I noticed we were packed in like sardines. Fully loaded, the boat was sitting in the calm water, tied to the dock, with only a foot to spare before water came over the side to sink us. I instantly had fears we would sink before we got out of the harbor and even before we hit the rough sea. We sat in the hot sun for thirty minutes and finally began our trip, only to get a quarter of a mile into open water before the driver started to fear for our safety. He turned the boat around. We went back to the dock and switched to a larger boat that was still not big enough for the load it was carrying. Traveling at thirty-five miles an hour, with sixty people and all of the luggage, in a medium sized open boat, was a scary experience.

San Pedro is located to the north along the barrier reef that borders the entire country of Belize on the east side. It is a popular tourist spot for those wanting to have a Caribbean experience near a large barrier reef, and who are not interested in the backroads of the country. It was similar to other islands we had previously visited in the Caribbean with white sand beaches.

The hotels and homes in that area were painted pastel shades of yellow, pink, blue, green and white. Their tiled roofs were also many different colors. Occasionally, I noticed a thatched roof hut in the outlying areas. Not far off shore, we could see the waves crashing onto the barrier reef that rose to the surface, and between the shore and the reef we could see the water was shallow, aqua blue, clear and smooth. The most common way to get around was to walk, drive a golf cart, ride a bicycle or travel by boat taxi from pier to pier along the shoreline.

I tried to set up a tarpon fishing trip for the first morning, but it was too windy. Instead, we went on a glass bottom boat to the reef and spent a few hours snorkeling on the calm side.

We stopped at two different places and had two completely different experiences. The first place was a normal reef ten to fifteen feet deep. There were interesting coral heads and plenty of fish, but nothing out of the normal based on my past scuba diving trips. The second place was very different. It was called Shark Ray Alley, and there was a drop off trough down thirty-five feet with an opening in the reef to the ocean. There the water was much bluer and the fish were larger, more unusual and more plentiful. We saw a large spotted ray with a slender, pointed tail ten feet long. We also spotted a big snapper, that looked somewhat like a grouper, probably five feet long and weighing at least two hundred pounds. No sharks were seen, but I'm sure they were occasionally in the area. A few of the other colorful reef fish we saw were parrotfish, butterfly fish, angel fish and dark blue tangs.

We ate at many different restaurants during our stay in Belize and never got sick. That was unexpected and a welcome surprise. We were careful on our day trips in the outlying areas, and we stayed in some really nice places. Maybe that was helpful in avoiding the bad water. In general, the locals drank either rain water collected from their roofs in large cisterns or drank purified bottled water. Some of them drank the other water, but I'm sure their intestinal tracts had adjusted to the bacteria, and it didn't seem to bother them.

After a few days in San Pedro, we returned to the international airport in Belize City for our trip back to the United States. Our earlier boat ride had been such a scary experience; we decided to take a small plane, which held only ten people.

The flight was scheduled to take only fifteen minutes, but our pilot decided to make an extra stop along the way and land on

Caye Caulker. The runway there was only a flat, dirt field. We sat in the plane after landing, while the pilot talked to a guy who had come out to meet him from a small shack located at the edge of the woods. Through the pilot's open window, they exchanged small, brown paper bags. We didn't know what was happening, but decided it must have been a drug exchange.

We left Belize in eighty degree weather wearing only shorts and tee shirts. We had a few mosquito bites on our arms and legs. When we landed in North Carolina, it was freezing, and there was snow on the ground.

Overall, it was a great trip to a very different part of the world. Because of the warm climate, friendly people, outstanding accommodations and diverse geography, I would recommend it to anyone interested in an out-of-the-norm adventure. Maybe someday, we will again travel to that friendly Central American country.

"The biggest adventure you have
is to live the life
of your dreams."

Oprah Winfrey

Argentina, South America
September 2005

Trent told me about a charitable organization looking for volunteers to go to Argentina to dig for dinosaur fossils. Because dinosaurs had always interested me, I signed up and found myself on their second expedition team of the year, going to do field work in the Andes Mountains. I was to hunt through Triassic sediments in the foothills of those mountains and a nearby remote desert, with a group of scientists and a few other volunteers.

The Triassic era was the time from 250 million to 210 million years ago and was credited with the emergence from the seas of the very first land vertebrates, including all mammals, dinosaurs and primitive crocodiles. Popular scientific theory has believed all modern creatures eventually evolved from those early beginnings.

At the end of the Triassic era, there was a worldwide extinction and everything that survived to the next major time period was classified as having lived in the Jurassic era. The Jurassic time period began around 210 million years ago and lasted until 65 million years ago. The Jurassic was when dinosaurs grew to huge proportions, roamed the entire earth and dominated all land mammals. Sixty-five million years ago, all the large dinosaurs died out suddenly, maybe because of a meteor strike to the earth, and today only birds with their similar characteristics remain.

Much preparation was necessary for me before leaving North Carolina. There were many official forms to fill out and return to the sponsoring organization, including health information I had to obtain from my personal doctor. They wanted to make sure I was healthy enough to endure the expedition, along with being able to tolerate the desert environment of arid Argentina where we would be living in individual tents.

I went to Wilmington Health Care to see a special travel doctor. We eliminated the need for malaria pills, which I had taken two years earlier when I had traveled to Belize. At that time I was given a tetanus shot, so I didn't need to get a new one, but I did get a booster for hepatitis A protection. I found I needed one original shot and then sometime later would need another booster shot to receive long-term immunity. I was able to avoid other shots such as polio, cholera, and tuberculosis based on the doctor knowing exactly where I would be traveling.

I spent a lot of time before the trip reading books recommended by the scientists in charge of the expedition. Those books included *Hunting for Dinosaurs* and *The Mistaken Extinction.* I also watched television and gained knowledge from the Science channel, Discovery channel, Nova channel and a variety of National Geographic specials. Anything on the subject of science and nature interested me, and those sources were invaluable.

In addition, I made trips to two natural history museums. I found a few interesting books at a museum in southern California, named the Brea Tar Pits. Those books focused on the finding of dinosaur eggs in Mongolia in the 1920s. Because of civil unrest in that part of the world, the scientist who discovered that rich fossil graveyard in Mongolia was not allowed to go back after 1929. The government finally allowed other scientists to again explore the area in the early 1990s. On those recent expeditions, many new discoveries had been made.

During a trip to Connecticut, I spent a whole afternoon at the world famous Yale Peabody Natural History Museum. There were wonderful exhibits of rare fossils from around the world. In the late 1800s, a man named O.C. Marsh became engaged in a contest between himself and Edward Drinker Cope to see who could find the most different species of dinosaurs from around the world. Both men sent out teams to search in various locations, and a lot of the fossils located by O.C. Marsh's crew were displayed at the museum.

Friday, September 15th, I had a very exciting day. I traveled from Wilmington to Atlanta, then on to Buenos Aires. The overnight flight to Argentina took nine and a half hours. Out of Atlanta, I had been unable to reserve a business class seat. Because I had waited in line for a few hours and had paid an extra $130 to get "a good seat," the fellow at the ticket counter ended up assigning me what he said was "a special seat." It was 15C and sounded like a coach seat to me. To my surprise, it was truly a special seat, one out of six that were strictly for pilots and flight attendants. Upon finding my plush seat and immediately folding it back with the foot rest in the up position, I was asked by a passing flight attendant if I had the correct seat. I told her I was sure I was in 15C and showed her my boarding ticket. She said she had to go check, and I observed a puzzled look on her face. She never came back from the business class section where she was working. I guessed my assigned seat was acceptable to everyone.

There was a wall in front of me and a wall behind. In my section with six seats across, separated in twos by two aisles, there were three wall mounted, large televisions. The plane was the most up-to-date I had ever been on. I was having fun reclining in the best seat I'd ever had and was looking forward to my adventure.

Arrival at the Buenos Aires Airport was smooth and right on schedule. I arrived around 8:30 a.m., one hour ahead of Eastern Standard Time in Wilmington. Because the time of year was completely opposite from North America, I was greeted to a warm, sunny spring day. I had been able to sleep for six and a half hours on the plane.

Getting my fully stuffed duffle bag from baggage claim was easy. In the process, I met one of the other individuals who was to be a volunteer on my expedition. He was from Chicago and had been on my plane. He was scheduled to fly to San Juan, Argentina early the next morning, but I was to make the flight that evening. We agreed we would see each other on Saturday at the Alkazar Hotel in San Juan where we could talk more.

I could not locate an ATM machine to get pesos for cab fare, lunch or tipping, so I ended up going to a booth in the terminal where the lady in charge swore there was no extra cost to exchange U.S. dollars to pesos. She told me her booth was under the control of the airport and all the other booths, except for hers, charged an extra fee for conversion. After I got my money, I didn't know if that was a true statement or not, because I had expected more pesos than I received. I gave her $200 U.S. and received $524 in pesos. I had thought the conversion rate was .34 cents U.S. to every one peso. I decided what I received was close enough, so I let it go. (Later, I found out I should have received $564 pesos, if there had been no transaction fee.)

I ate lunch at the Café/Café while at the airport. The hamburger, fries and Pepsi I ordered really hit the spot. The cost was fifteen pesos including a mandatory tip of two pesos. I was in no hurry, because my ten hour layover left me all the time I needed. I had fun placing the food order and working out the payment, before I sat by myself for hours and read a book.

My first attempt at using the pre-paid phone card was not successful. I could not understand the directions on the telecom machines, and none of the codes seemed to work. Even after asking a few people in the airport, including an airport security guard, I still had no success. Later on, after taking a 60 peso taxi ride to another airport, New Berry, for my next flight, I was finally able to get the pre-paid phone card to work. Trent had asked me to call her after I arrived in South America. I knew she was glad I called to let her know I had arrived safely. I tried to speak to her some of my newly acquired Spanish. All she did was laugh, but it was worth the effort to me.

At the New Berry Airport, I caught my final plane to San Juan. I had hoped to check into the Alkazar Hotel around 9:30 that night. Between the three flights and all the layover time in-between, I had traveled constantly for one and a half days. That still didn't include the 200 mile truck trip I needed to take through the desert, on bad roads, to arrive at my final destination. I couldn't wait to set up my one-man tent there.

When I arrived at the airport in San Juan on Saturday evening, there was a man standing by the door with a sign for the Alkazar Hotel. I was pleased to see him, and found he was waiting for me. He helped me load my duffle bag, sleeping bag and backpack in his van for the fifteen mile ride to the hotel. It was 9:00 at night as we drove along, and people in the town were walking everywhere. I later found out most of them didn't eat supper until around 10:00 and then stayed up late each night.

After asking my driver if he spoke English, and him replying, "No comprenda," I knew I had better just sit back and enjoy the ride.

On my last two-hour plane ride, I had sat next to a lady who lived in San Juan and was going home. She tried to talk to me, and I tried to talk to her, without much success. I tried some of the phrases I had learned from my Spanish book and CDs I had studied before starting the trip. Even though she understood some of them, I couldn't understand her replies.

When I stood to exit the plane, I remembered the phrase for "good evening," which was "buenos noches," and I spoke that phrase to her in an attempt at saying goodbye.

She understood, smiled and repeated back to me, "Buenos noches."

I checked in at the hotel, and my luggage was taken to the room for me. My room was on the fourth floor overlooking the city. Going through the door, I quickly realized the room was very hot. I asked the gentleman how to turn on the air conditioner. I pointed to an air vent on the wall, because I couldn't find anything else in the room that resembled an air conditioner.

His reply was what I was getting used to hearing, "No comprenda."

When I pointed to the vent, he pointed to some controls on the wall and shook his head up and down. After tipping him, he left the room, probably smiling. As hot as the room was already, when I turned on the controls, it was quickly obvious they only operated the heater. I went over to the windows and, to my relief, all of them opened. As the cool night air rushed past me into the room, I stood on the fourth floor five stories above the city streets. All of the night noise of cars honking, changing gears and people talking, flowed up to my window. I could see across the city from one end to the other. San Juan had turned out to be a larger, more modern place than I had expected. The nearby mountain ranges just outside the city were not obvious, until I woke up the next morning and looked out the window again.

I then took a quick walk down the hallway to check out the staircase going to the lobby. I had read that the city of San Juan was located near a large geological fault line near the Andes Mountains. In 1944, all the buildings of the city were destroyed in an earthquake, and thousands of people were killed. I wanted to know my whereabouts to have a quick exit from the building, if it started shaking during the night.

Back in the room the phone rang and a lady said, "I don't speak very much English, but you have a Mr. Frank waiting for you in the restaurant downstairs."

When I tried to ask some simple questions, she replied, "No comprenda."

I looked at my list of people going on the expedition. There was nobody by the name of Frank, so I decided she must have the wrong room number. I didn't want to be flimflammed after having just arrived. I quickly settled down for nine hours of sleep.

In the morning, I cleaned up, took a long shower and went to the first floor restaurant for their buffet breakfast. While enjoying fruit, sliced ham and hard bread, I overheard a conversation in the nearby lobby. Standing there was an older, grey haired gentleman talking to two fellows who had just arrived with the same type bags I had. I caught just enough of the conversation to know they were part of my expedition team.

I finished my breakfast and walked over to introduce myself.

One of them turned out to be Mr. Frank, and we had a good laugh about him not being able to communicate effectively to me through the desk clerk.

He and two men from Team One, from the previous two weeks, were planning to go to the museum in San Juan where all the dinosaur fossils were shipped after each expedition.

I was asked, "Would you like to come along?"

I replied, "You bet I would!"

We walked a mile through the city on our way to the museum. On the way, I asked many questions about their experiences during the past two weeks while they were in the Andes Mountains looking for fossils.

Mr. Frank said, "I have been on two of the different expeditions each year for the past eleven years. One of these fellows has been on five of them with me."

That information in itself was interesting to know. To find out that the trip was enough fun and educational enough to return more than once, was encouraging.

Mr. Frank then said, "It's a different trip each time. We never know what we'll find when we go out there."

As the conversation kicked off, I learned that during the last two weeks in the field it had snowed enough on a few of the days to cause trouble prospecting for bones. It had actually shut Team One down for three days, and everyone had just hung out around the campsite. For a week, the temperature dropped to 24 degrees each night, and the snow was mixed with rain and sleet. Two of the team members had been so unprepared for the extreme weather, they decided to quit after the first week. They were then driven to a small settlement two hours away where they caught a small bus to San Juan. From San Juan, they flew home early. I was told those conditions were not normal for September, because that month was supposed to begin their springtime.

We arrived at the museum and were allowed access on a Saturday during a time it was normally closed. I entered the front doors and saw mounted displays of some of the dinosaurs, mammals and prehistoric crocodiles found in the region we would soon visit. Dates of roughly 235 to 220 million years ago were placed next to most of the skeletons. I took some flash photos in the open halls where the large skeletons were assembled. There was one large carnivore in the main hall that stood twelve feet tall and looked like a T. Rex, but I'm not sure which name it was given there in Argentina. On the other side of the hall was a Herrarasaurus, which was a smaller carnivore that looked mean with long teeth, big jaws and curled claws. Beside it was a smaller mounted Oeraptor. That species had only been discovered in the last ten years and predated most of the others to about 235 million years ago. It was credited as being one of the first dinosaurs.

We walked past other exhibits to see a few fellows who worked at the museum busy assembling a mount. It was a cast that would show the dinosaur as it had looked with muscle, skin and eyes. I found out those guys also worked on removing hard sediment encased around groups of fossils brought in from the field. That type of work was usually done during the months when the weather did not permit teams to go out and excavate.

I was allowed to go into some of the back rooms to view other skeletons being worked on. There was one about the size of an African rhino and another one called a Cynadont, which was a vertebrate that survived the major extinction at the end of the Triassic around 210 million years ago. It was supposed to resemble a dog and lived in burrows in the ground to avoid the larger carnivores. It was the creature to which humans supposedly owed their existence, due to future evolution and the continuation of other vertebrate creatures. I found it all to be very interesting.

In one of the rooms, there were many boxes of food which, I was told, would be consumed by our team over the next two weeks. I learned that in Team Two there would be more than the original nine members. I only knew of six volunteers and two scientists, but I found out there were additional graduate students and a few employees from the museum planning to make the expedition with us.

As we left the building and walked back across town, my excitement began to build. I had not counted on getting to see the museum or to run into others from Team One who had been excavating for the last two weeks.

We experienced a mild 75 degree sunny afternoon on the way to a street side café, as I asked other questions. It led to discovering that Team Two would be exploring a whole new region. Only during the last few days, Team One had found a canyon from aerial photographs that the team leader was sure had never been explored. Team One had traveled over to its edge on the last day of their stay, a two hour drive through the rough desert from base camp, and tried to locate a way to safely reach the valley floor some 800 feet straight below. I looked at some digital photos on one of the men's camera, and in the photos he stood on the canyon's edge looking down. In the background, the drop-off looked like the Grand Canyon in North America. Very scary! From what I saw, I wasn't sure if the trip was going to be too extreme, even for me.

As we walked back to the hotel, one of the men told a story about last year's expedition to the same area. It was interesting and a little scary. He said that in a town halfway between San Juan and where we would set up camp, some 130 miles northwest in the desert, someone spread the word that people from the museum had been stealing fossils from the area. It was published in their newspaper, so the people of that town were very angry.

When the expedition finished its two-week stay in the desert, and the members of the team passed through the town of Valle Fertil, the local police arrested all of them. All the vehicles, fossils and gear were confiscated. After hours of waiting and being searched, the volunteers were finally allowed to leave. The team leader, Oscar, then spent weeks straightening out the mess and finally got all of the stuff back. Apparently, that disagreement had settled down, because we were scheduled to travel through that same town both going and returning.

I learned Oscar resigned from his position as Director of Talampaya National Park during the year as a result of that harassment. Our teams had obtained special permission to do the scientific dinosaur digs from the government for the benefit of science and museums in Argentina. Oscar and his dinosaur expeditions were originally a part of the reason the area had been established as a national park. There were plans to possibly expand the park based on his new findings.

A few hours later, I was to meet the entire Team Two members downstairs in the lobby. I had been told we would travel across town to a very nice restaurant where we would enjoy fine Argentinean wine and one pound steaks with all the trimmings. One of last week's expedition members had described that routine outing as quite a feast. He told me to eat a few early snacks, because the meal would not start until 10:00 p.m. and would end around 1:00 a.m.

At 9:00 p.m. we left in three taxis, costing four pesos per car, and traveled to Oscar's favorite restaurant. We were seated at a long table, and almost none of the volunteers knew what he was ordering from the menu because it was written in Spanish. The fellow next to me thought he was ordering soup, and it turned out to be some form of thick gravy. Even though we tried to communicate with the waiter, when we pointed to a menu item to question him, he would just write it down as if that's what we wanted to order. What we received turned out to be a big grab bag of strange dishes.

My food was good. It was a sandwich on thick bread with sliced steak, ham and cheese. My attempt to order a salad with tomatoes turned out to be all green lettuce with no tomatoes, but a fellow down the way got half lettuce and half tomatoes filling his plate. He really didn't know what he was ordering. The wine served was "all you can drink," and I overdid it. It was a Mendoza Malbec from Argentina and contained a mixture of two different red grapes. It was delicious, and I kept the label from the bottle. Everyone kicked in forty pesos to cover the cost of their meal with tip included. That was about $16.00 U.S. and a big bargain. I was told we would be back to the same restaurant on our final night in two weeks to celebrate.

As we left the restaurant, we were given instructions to be in the lobby, packed and ready to go, at 7:00 in the morning. I was very excited and could hardly wait.

That morning, I checked out of the hotel after taking my last bath for the next two weeks. We were driven from the lobby to the museum entrance. There we loaded the truck with what looked to be enough food for a month. We were told we would be allowed to eat all we wanted, at any time, during the trip. That was good news.

Once loaded, I noticed the tires on the double cab pickup truck in which I would be riding. They were almost flat in the back from the excess weight, and three of the four tires had the steel belts showing through the rubber from excessive wear. I was concerned if we would be able to safely make the trip, because seven people and all our gear still had to be loaded. I found out a smaller pickup truck, that was to hold four people, had also been rented for the trip. Later, it was completely loaded.

We left the museum and went directly to a gas station to fill the tires with air and get gas which cost about $4.00 U.S. per gallon.

After we were thirty minutes out of town and heading for our destination, I asked how long it would take to get to base camp. I was told seven hours, if nothing went wrong. That would turn out to be an understatement. I saw a sign that stated the area of Ischigualasto was 300 kilometers, or about 200 miles, away. I knew that area was reasonably close to where we were going.

We had probably already traveled 50 miles by the time I asked the question.

The first part of the trip was on good, paved highway. We were traveling way too fast at 75 miles an hour. I was truly expecting a tire to blow at any time. That had me nervous most of the way.

Midway into the trip, one of the guys said he would like to stop, use the bushes for a bathroom break, and take a few photos of the snow covered mountains and unusual terrain. We stopped, and as we climbed out, we began to hear steam coming from the radiator. That was bad news! Upon raising the hood, we discovered that somehow, during our trip, the radiator fan had become completely detached from the engine. The fan was damaged and had wedged itself between the radiator and the engine block, hanging on by just one blade. Because it was no longer cooling, the engine had become severely overheated.

The smaller vehicle that had been following us stopped, and together we evaluated the situation. It was decided we needed extra tools and plenty of water for the radiator. The smaller truck was then loaded with as many people as it could hold, and it left to go on down the road to the campsite, with the driver promising to return in a few hours with the necessary items.

Those who were left, including me, unloaded all the gear and food in the back, in order to reach some simple tools that were stored there. We ended up removing the guards around the radiator, retrieving the fan, beating out the bent blades with a hammer and praying it would work when replaced. Two and a half hours later, three gallons of water that had arrived from the base camp were added to the radiator. Later, all went smoothly, but we stopped five times to check the fan and radiator on our way to the camp that evening.

The last ten kilometers were over extremely rough terrain. The smaller vehicle picked up a large thorn in the front tire somewhere along the way. When we tried to pull it out, the air started escaping. The thorn was left in place because we didn't have a plug to fix it. There were a few times in the gullies, which had washed through the roadbed, when I thought we were stuck. After everyone bailed out and pushed, we got the truck going forward again.

We reached the campsite, and everyone picked his own spot in the sand, separated by bushes to block off the winds. We set up our own tents. The soil in the area was dark red sand and clay with many small rocks mixed into it. We were told everything we owned would be red by the time the trip ended.

By the time I went through my bags and organized some of my belongings on the tent floor, it was dark outside. It had been quite a day! The trip to get there had taken ten hours, and I realized I had been traveling off and on for the past four days just to finally arrive at our campsite in the desert. One of those days had been spent in San Juan, where I relaxed and walked through the city to kill time. That had been a nice break from all the hours of traveling. I also thought about the fact that in two weeks I would be repeating the whole process in reverse on my return trip home.

At nine o'clock on the first night, we gathered around a big campfire and ate Argentinean beef by flashlight. It was complimented by big helpings of steamed onions, eggplant, and green peppers that had all been grilled with the steaks. There was plenty of red wine to drink and that made it a complete feast. Using my flashlight, I went to my tent around midnight. The moon was full and illuminated the foothills we were soon to explore. It was very cold, and it had been since the sun had gone down. It just hadn't been obvious while we were eating and sitting close to the campfire. I would guess the daytime temperature was in the upper 90s and at night it dipped to around 35 degrees. There had been no snow yet as the last group had experienced, and for that I was glad.

On Monday, we were looking for an eventful first day of

prospecting. The day started off with a light breakfast at 8:00. Afterward, Oscar had us assemble for an orientation. He was a nice guy, along with his scientist friend, Ricardo. We received our first rules about what we could and couldn't do. In general, everything was to be somewhat loose. We were told we would have a lot of freedom in the field and around the campfire. We could eat just about anything we wanted, whenever we wanted. There was a short talk about the geology of the whole region. Oscar laid out a large, colored satellite map showing different places we would be searching over the next two weeks. Most of the sediment would be between 210 and 225 million years old.

Our team was to be focused more on the middle Triassic time-frame, where the first team had searched much older sediments from 230 to 240 million years old. During the second week of our trip, Oscar announced that a world specialist in paleo-magnetic science would be joining us. He would be drilling core samples to help date the entire region to within five hundred thousand years, instead of the wide range of time we were currently working with. His magnetic core samples would also compare Argentina to Europe and North America from the time of Pangaea, when all the continents were still connected in one large land mass.

Before we started out for the day, I decided it was time for me to give "the shovel and a good view" a first try. Digging a hole was no problem, but trying to balance over it with my pants down and squatting was a little tricky. I accomplished the task without falling backward into the hole and was soon ready to leave camp. We had been instructed to bury all evidence, along with the toilet paper. There was seldom a rain shower in the desert, and if left uncovered, the toilet paper would blow in the wind for months, or even up to a year, before it finally disappeared.

I boarded Ricardo's truck along with eight others. We fish-tailed out of the campsite onto an extremely rough, sandy, clay road, while weaving between the desert broom bushes. Everyone was laughing and having a good time until Ricardo looked in the rearview mirror and noticed Frank had fallen off the back and was lying in the middle of the road. No one had seen Frank climb on the back bumper. We were later told Frank, a 74 year old man, had been on other expeditions with these two scientists, and had been allowed to ride the back bumper while holding the back door handle, during the slow parts of the trip through the sand and gullies. On that morning, Ricardo didn't know Frank was riding in that fashion. We were going much too fast and taking the corners with speed. He just couldn't hold on.

We rushed back to Frank, who was dazed and covered in red dust. Ricardo apologized over and over. Frank was a very nice man, in great physical shape, and reminded everyone of Indiana Jones in the movies. We dusted him off, and he climbed in the truck so we could continue our trip to the foothills six miles away. The rest of the trip was slow, through washed out river-beds with many deep ruts. I believe I could have walked as fast as we were moving.

We arrived at the spot chosen for the day. After getting out, we were told to report back in five hours, around 4:00 p.m. We were instructed to search up to two miles in any direction. I set my GPS, marking the spot of the truck, and started out with five others. Ricardo led us for a short distance, and told us he wanted to find a bone in order to show us what we would be looking for.

After fifteen minutes, Lou, another member of the team, found a 5″ piece of bone in a narrow ravine. As he was showing it to Ricardo, I walked up the hillside and discovered two large vertebra bones lying on the surface. I brushed off some of the dust and told Ricardo what I had located. We immediately marked the spot with the GPS for later excavation. I thought the bones were very interesting, and my excitement began to build. Those two bones were four inches in diameter. I noted the color of the preserved bone, so I could identify others in the future.

About that time, everyone decided to split up, and we went

off in different directions. I picked a landmark consisting of a large hill and bluff that dropped off quickly to set a waypoint on my GPS, as it was a location close to the parked truck where we were to meet later in the day. I knew that landmark would stand out in the mountain range from a few miles away and would serve as a backup to my GPS and the small compass connected to my watchband.

As I wandered up and down small hills covered with loose rocks, I checked my compass constantly. That gave me a degree of confidence as to where I was, because I knew how easy it would be to become disoriented, since all the small hills and valleys looked the same.

By midday, I began to get warm, so I took off my long sleeve sweater I had worn through the night. Within an hour, I discovered another dinosaur bone. It turned out to be a medium sized femur, or upper leg bone. It was broken in three places and overall was twelve inches long. All the pieces fit together perfectly, even though they were originally scattered down the hillside over a four foot distance. I marked the location with my GPS and searched the whole area, but found no more bones showing above the ground.

The rest of the afternoon was spent walking, while staying very focused on the ground for small items of interest. I visited some of the sites where others had found bones. Not many finds were very exciting because most were just bone fragments. Oscar and Ricardo were both excited about the spot overall, because two years earlier it was close to where four completely new dinosaur species had been located. Oscar told us the year of 2003 had been very productive. Those finds were important, because everything found would eventually help to bridge the gap in knowledge of early evolution during the very first immergence of primitive life.

Supper that night was great. Three people, including myself, sliced onions, green peppers and olives, grated some cheese, and using tomato sauce made four large pizzas on large circles of bread that were originally planned for some other use. We cooked all of it on an open fire using hot coals and a metal grating. We also served spaghetti, with a wonderful sauce, made from some of the same ingredients that had been stirred into a big black pot heated by the campfire. We heated a loaf of Italian bread and served it with slices of cheese. With the red and white wine, everyone thought the meal was great and gave us a big toast.

On Tuesday, the day started at 7:00 in the morning. I cleaned myself up with a wet rag and ate some crackers, jelly, peanut butter, sliced ham and fruit around 8:00. We were out in the field by 9:00. The weather was so pleasant, I wore only a short sleeve tee shirt and light vest.

That day we started off at the same location as the day before in the Los Colorados Formation. The difference was we walked much farther from where the truck was parked. I probably covered over five miles through rough terrain. There were alternating hills and valleys, very close together. The focus for everyone was to look closely in the red clay of the steep hillsides. Erosion by wind and water, during the rainy season of winter, constantly broke down the soil and it exposed more bones and skeletons.

Everyone became frustrated after two hours, because no one was finding anything. I was the exception. About midday, I had located two pieces of bone in a drainage ditch dropping down off a hillside. The bones fit together perfectly for a fifteen inch tibia, as explained by Ricardo. He was excited about the find, collected the specimen and recorded its location on his GPS. All of the other searchers came over for a look. They intensified their search of the immediate area, but didn't find anything else. After everyone finally walked off in different directions, I walked with Ricardo, and he talked about the find. He had a good idea from its size and shape of the exact species of dinosaur to which it belonged.

We walked together an additional hundred yards, and I noticed another bone on a hillside. We both got down on our knees for a closer look. It was broken in half but much thicker than the first bone I had found. As he was checking it out, I found the second part of it buried a few feet away. With both pieces together, he said it was a nice femur from the same type of dinosaur we had found earlier. Again, he documented that additional bone, collected it in his bag and marked its location on his GPS. I had to sign his book as the finder of both bones. No others were found close by.

As we walked away he said, "Both of those bones were good finds. You certainly have a good eye for what we are doing."

We then traveled a mile away to a location near a cliff face where others were excavating a skeleton first located in 2003. Oscar explained that originally only the tailbones were exposed, but as they had dug farther down in the sediment, they continued to find bones. I was told there was big hope for that find, and maybe its complete excavation would carry into the next season. A truck was used to get as close as possible. Then some of the men carried a generator over to the area to run a jackhammer. The skeleton was embedded in some very hard sediment.

The next day, Wednesday, we started out on foot from the base camp and walked toward a large range of mountains a mile away. We were told to search the narrow ledges as high up as we felt safe. I started off by climbing one hundred feet up off the valley floor on a narrow three foot wide ledge and then traveled horizontally and upwards. It was hard to do, because the sediment levels were all slanted dramatically upward, caused by volcanic eruptions from over millions of years. There were many washed out gullies close together, and the loose sandy soil was full of small round stones that caused me to constantly slip downhill with each step. Three of the guys maneuvered up the cliff face above me three hundred feet from the valley floor. The hillside was so vertical, I couldn't understand how they had climbed so high once they got there.

After an hour, one of the volunteers named John yelled down that he had found a bone. The other two guys were soon clustered around him in an effort to see it from a narrow, slanted ledge. I decided to scale the slope to get a look at their discovery. Finally, I got five yards below it and looked up to see on the surface a leg bone fifteen inches long. It was broken in six pieces that were still lined up perfectly. It did look like a nice find.

I slowly managed to return to a lower, safer level and kept up my search. During the late morning and hot afternoon, I covered five to six miles. A lot of that was up and down very steep hillsides. In the late afternoon, as my legs began to tire, I decided it was no longer safe for me to be searching at those heights so close to the edge. I also realized I was out of drinking water and was getting very thirsty working in the direct sun. We were supposed to meet back at the campsite at 5:00, but I hung around while Oscar and Ricardo scaled the hillside and took a look at the bone on the upper ledge that had been found earlier that day.

As I looked some three hundred feet upward, I could tell they were very excited. Oscar carefully dug out around the leg bone and discovered part of a pelvis, some vertebras and other bones. It was not a complete dinosaur, but a very good find. The small group of individuals yelled down for me to come up and take a closer look. Even though I was very tired, I scaled the mountain and was breathing hard as I neared the fossil. I had left my heavy backpack in the valley below and only carried my camera. The find was on such a vertical slope, in loose soil, that I had to carefully place each foot. I got within two feet and took a few photos. Quickly, I backed away and worked toward a safer ledge to rest. Oscar and Ricardo said those bones had "made their day." They would later be taking them back to the museum in plaster casts.

The site was marked by GPS, and a piece of white toilet paper was put under a rock close by as a marker. Another group of workers would come by later and put a linen and plaster cast jacket around the three foot area, before an attempt would be made to get the group of bones down the steep mountain face. I hoped I was not the one asked to help with that task. The danger seemed too great to me.

No other major finds were made. There were some bone fragments at other spots on the same level, but most were not considered "keepers." Fossil hunting for me had turned into hard work. I had the feeling I would sleep soundly that night.

I was so hungry when I got back to camp, I ate a cup full of green olives, two oranges, and a raw green pepper. I was betting supper would be tasty around 10:00.

I returned to my tent after the long day of searching the cliffs and pulled off my shoes and socks. My feet and lower legs were red from the soil, as were my arms and face. I noticed I was developing blisters on my left heel and both big toes. The soil was so loose it was like walking in sand on the beach. By constantly pushing off with my toes, there was excess friction inside my shoes. Even though I had worn two pairs of special hiking socks, I had to bandage both of my big toes with moleskin. There were many small stones mixed in with the red clay and sand. That made it exceptionally hard to keep my balance when climbing up an incline. It seemed like I was slipping backward one step for every two steps I moved forward.

The next day we traveled in two trucks for two hours across the flat flood plain, bumping from one washed out gully to the next. It was slow going for fifteen miles as we covered the distance. We finally arrived at the very edge of a sheer drop 800 feet to a canyon floor. It was the place they had told me about on my first day, that the earlier team had discovered.

Twelve of us piled out of the trucks. We started climbing one of the nearby ridges that rose steeply upward, with only a few feet to spare from the edge, in an effort to find a good place to make a descent.

One of the volunteers said he had to slow down because of the extreme elevation. I checked my GPS. We were at 4,220 feet of altitude, and the incline was going upwards rapidly.

We finally reached a steep ledge where Oscar and Ricardo, a few graduate students, and two volunteers decided to go down with ropes and picks. We were all given the choice of whether to attempt the descent to the canyon floor for bone prospecting, or go back down the hill and prospect a rolling valley with over-hangs. I chose the rolling valley. As I took pictures of the group heading down the canyon wall, all I could do was shake my head. What they were about to do was way too extreme for anyone ex-cept trained professionals with better climbing gear. At the time, I was unsure if some of those people would return alive.

I spent the whole afternoon in the rolling valley prospecting a combination of volcanic grey ash and dark red Triassic sedi-ment with no success. There were four others with me, and we covered two square miles by spreading out. We had our GPS devices set to know the location of the parked trucks. Everyone, from both groups, was given instructions to be back there at 4:00 in the afternoon.

Just to be safe, I arrived back at the trucks around 3:30. Frank was already sprawled out in the shade of an overhanging ridge with his hat over his face. It didn't take me long to get in the same position. All of the others, who had started out with me for the day, appeared by 4:00. They were dragging from the heat, because of all the walking they had done while carrying back-packs that weighed at least thirty pounds.

We waited patiently until 5:00, and then I became worried something had gone wrong with the other group who had gone down the vertical wall into the valley. There was no one visible on the far cliff's edge a quarter of a mile away. They were an hour late. Frank told me to give them until 6:00, so we just wait-ed. At 5:45, I told everyone I would walk to the top where we had been earlier in the morning and see if anyone could be seen climbing up the canyon wall. Frank and John went with me, but quit halfway because they were too tired.

We worked out two signals I would give with my arms. Two arms raised over my head and touching at the hands in the shape of a big "O" was the signal everything was fine. If I raised both arms in a crossed fashion, Frank was to leave in one of the trucks below and go back to our campsite for help. We really didn't know exactly what help he could find, and we knew it would be getting dark soon. We were not even totally sure if Frank could find his way back to the base camp through the desert after dark.

As I approached the final one hundred yards of the upward slope and neared the spot the others had climbed down, my heart was beating quickly. I was really hoping for the best, but because of the late time of the evening, I figured something had not gone as planned. As I glanced over the edge, I saw three Argentinean students coming up the last fifty yards, climbing hand over hand, using a long white rope.

I couldn't communicate very well with them, but I tried any-way as they reached the crest. I asked, "Is everyone OK?"

One of them understood me and replied in English, "They are fine."

I then asked, "Where is everyone else?"

He turned and pointed down the steep cliff face to the valley far below. As I stared down, I could barely see the small group of tiny people on the valley floor looking upward. They were waiting at the bottom until the younger students made it to the top. In that the younger Argentineans had successfully made the assent, it was now their turn to attempt the long climb upward. At that moment, I was very glad I had not gone down the cliff with them.

I turned and gave the OK signal to Frank standing a quarter of a mile away by forming a big "O" above my head with my arms. I was sure he was relieved. I could see him turn and deliver the message to the rest of the waiting group farther on down the hill.

The three young students motioned for me to follow them. As we started moving down the hill quickly toward the trucks, the one who spoke English said, "We need to leave soon."

By the time I arrived at the truck, everyone was loaded, the truck was running and they shouted, "Get in!"

Off we went toward the base camp. I was told the others would pack themselves in the smaller truck when they got to the top some forty-five minutes later. Hopefully, it would not be totally dark by that time, so they could see to climb to the top of the cliff.

As it turned out, the bigger truck didn't have working headlights. The reason we had been in such a hurry was that we were following the tire ruts in the sand we had made that morning when we arrived. We needed to get back to camp before dark. We bumped along at a snail's pace and arrived at base camp just as it was getting so dark we could hardly see the tire tracks.

The smaller truck finally showed up in camp an hour and a half later with the headlights shining brightly and its horn blaring loudly. I could hear cheers of joy from everyone aboard as they reached the campsite in the dark. There were many stories told that night around the campfire having to do with the day's activities. A sign was hung by the lantern that read, "Zero dead–September 22." It had been an "unbelievable" day.

I was up by 6:45 on Friday. I washed my hair in a big bowl, shaved, put Band-Aids on my two blisters, and ate cheese and hard bread with a little jelly. The meal the night before had been prepared quickly, but the chicken, potato, and onion stew tasted good to all the hungry souls, along with the white and red wine.

Oscar said we would again walk to an open area a few miles from camp, because there had been some really nice finds a few days earlier on a high cliff. They needed to enclose the best one of those finds in a plaster jacket and get it down off the mountain. Everyone was told to prospect on the steep edges of the canyon walls. Fortunately, they were not quite as steep as the day before.

I started off by myself in a new direction, and decided I would just take it slow. The ground everywhere had been pushed upward at odd angles by past volcanic activity. Where one level of strata would start at ground level, it might end up some 700 to 800 feet higher. I followed one of those levels upward and marked a few GPS waypoints, as I weaved in and out around large boulders and ravines running irregularly down the mountainside. I was going slowly as I looked around for bones. Each ledge seemed to lead to something more inviting. I followed the edge of a large outcropping on my way up, because that was the type of area where some good finds had been made in recent days. Above me were huge boulders of red rock that cast a nice shadow and shielded the hot sun. I was just hoping there would not be an earthquake while I was climbing, because I was located near a major fault line that ran through the mountains.

After two hours, I found my way to the very top of that mountain. As I looked out over the ridges, I could see another part of the snowcapped Andes Mountains in the distance. A single Andean condor was sailing in the breeze above my head, and I spotted a flock of eight blue-green parrots flying together far down in the valley. Highly visible sediment levels of various thicknesses lined all the canyon walls across the valley. The warm sun enhanced the dark red color of everything for miles around. The sky was very blue with no visible clouds, and even though the air was cool at the moment, I knew it would get much warmer as the day progressed.

I had a feeling of complete isolation and a sensation of superiority in that I had found a way to the very top. I was a little concerned about making the trip back down later in the day, carrying my forty-pound backpack. On the way up, with a pick, I had cut hand and foot holds into the cliff face to help my climb. The vertical descent down would be much harder.

On the top of the mountain, I discovered a large area of rolling terrain that was fairly flat and seemed to extend for over a mile.

It looked to be the perfect spot to find some dinosaur bones. Off I went, constantly keeping sight of a large, unusual rock I had climbed around as I reached the crest. I used that as my major landmark, so I could later find my way down. I checked my GPS, and it showed an altitude of 4,958 feet. It scared me a little, because I didn't want to get lost or hurt that far from base camp since no one knew where I was searching.

I knew the air was thin at that altitude, but it didn't seem to be bothering me much. I just decided to take it easy, drink a lot of water and constantly monitor my location using the GPS. I set an additional waypoint on my GPS at a new landmark. I checked the location of the sun in the sky, and my compass was checked against both. I wanted to be sure to find that spot when I was ready to start back down later in the afternoon.

I found some isolated bones very quickly, but nothing big. Because of the distance I had traveled, I decided to pick up a few of the larger ones and take them to Oscar back at camp, so he could make a decision about whether the area was worth exploring further. I marked the site by GPS. That way I could later find the exact location if needed.

As the day progressed, it got warmer. I drank plenty of water and ate a lunch of ham, cheese and hard bread. About 2:30, I decided it was time to head back down. That went well since I took my time, but it was not easy. When I reached the area for my vertical downward climb, I moved very slowly and carefully placed my feet and hands into the groves I had cut in the rock on the way up, before shifting my weight. I knew I had to concentrate on every move. Other areas involved maneuvering around boulders and working my way through large washed out ravines that plunged down the mountainside many hundreds of feet below.

Finally, on the valley floor, I walked along the trail of my earlier footprints in the red sand on my way back toward the camp. I had a feeling of relief at having survived the tough climb and to again be on flat, safe ground. After a mile walking through the valley floor, I noticed five people up on a hillside extracting a set of bones in a fresh plaster cast. They saw me walking from hundreds of feet above and yelled for me to come up and see what they were doing. I dropped my heavy backpack, removed my camera and started climbing.

As I neared their location, I could see one white plaster jacket drying in the sun. Everyone was clustered around the spot of extraction. I was told there was more of the skeleton still running back into the hillside. I took some photos and helped them pick out the hard red rock around the remaining skeleton. The spot looked to be one area Oscar and Ricardo, along with other helpers, would continue working on for a few more days. They told me the main bones already encased in the plaster cast were spectacular.

The next morning we were up at 4:00 in a heavy rain. Originally, I hadn't thought too much about it, but the raindrops hitting the top of the tent had kept me awake during the night. I thought it was sleeting, since that had happened two weeks earlier with the first team.

At breakfast Oscar told us how afraid he had become during the night when he heard it raining. We had the camp set up in a flat valley bordered on each side by huge mountains. The valley was a major flood plain during the rainy season. In choosing the spot for the main campsite, Oscar had felt sure it was late enough in the spring that no more rain would fall. He told us to move all of the individual tents to higher ground, because the water draining off the mountains could rise very quickly where we were located. Off in the distance, the skies were very dark. It would rain hard for a while, and then the cold wind would blow.

I immediately leveled off a space on a nearby hillside and dragged my tent there. Once staked down, I piled dirt and stones around the entire outside edges. I had been told that when the wind kicked up into a Zonda, it could get under the tent and potentially blow it away.

With everyone's tent moved, we gathered around the fire to try and stay warm. Oscar said we would stay at camp that day, in case we needed to quickly move the main tent which contained all the food, extra supplies and firewood.

We started out trying to make a simple lunch of green pea soup from instant soup packages. The soup's ingredients grew and grew as everyone jumped in to help. Eventually, we enjoyed soup with peas, carrots, potatoes and chicken pieces that were all cooked in a big black pot. I cut up a huge amount of onions and potatoes that were fried in an iron skillet. Others fixed five large pizzas with everything you could imagine for toppings. Outside of the tomato sauce, pizza bread, onions and green peppers, they added olives, spicy peppers, sausage and fat back bacon slices. It was a very good meal and a different kind of lunch.

The weather cleared somewhat after lunch, but the blowing wind kept it cold. We were all bored just sitting around the fire. I remembered the interesting bones I had found the previous day at the top of the mountain. I had planned to show them to Oscar and Ricardo during the prior evening, but had forgotten and left them in my tent. I walked over to my tent and retrieved them.

When I showed them to Oscar and Ricardo, Oscar said to me, "Where did you find those?"

I described the unusual place, and how I had found the bones by traveling up the canyon edge while following the layers of sediment.

Oscar then asked, "Can you show us the place?"

"Yes," I replied.

He said quickly, "Let's go!"

Eleven people at the campsite grabbed their backpacks and off we went. It took the group close to two hours to climb to the spot, while I led. When we rounded the last ridge, we were thousands of feet higher than the valley floor and some two miles from the campsite. We then walked across the large rolling plains at the top.

Ricardo told me the site looked wonderful. Everyone was

instructed to fan out, and we all walked in different directions and began to search for bones. It wasn't long before I heard shouts that other bones had been found. As I went from spot to spot, which the other volunteers marked by putting white toilet paper under the edge of small rocks, I was amazed. There were complete leg bones, scattered vertebras, rib bones and all kinds of neat things being found. The area we were searching was large and would surely take a few days, with everyone looking, to really get an idea of what it truly held.

Later on, when we all arrived back at the campsite, I was the hero of the day. Oscar told me he was excited about future exploring at that location. Some of the volunteers started calling the top of that ridge "Hearn Mountain."

The next day, Sunday, would be a day of rest. Everyone slept until 8:00 and then ate a good breakfast.

At noon, everyone loaded into the two trucks. We drove through rained out gullies toward Talampaya National Park thirty miles away. It turned out to be a wonderful day of adventure, and it gave the blisters on my three toes a chance to recover. As we first entered the park, there was a check station that served food. I ordered, at the suggestion of one of my Argentinean friends, a thin steak with ham and cheese on a toasted slice of bread. With that sandwich, I ordered Quilmes (pronounced Kill-mes) beer, because it was a good beer served throughout Argentina. The meal was delicious and the cost was less than ten pesos.

Our entire group was allowed to take the guided tour through the park for free, because we were part of the expedition that would ultimately increase the size of the park based on the importance of our scientific findings. Normally, the admission price was twenty-five pesos per person. The park included a very special formation of cliffs that towered straight up off the valley floor for 600 feet. From a distance, the edges of the walls looked to have been sculpted with smooth upward channels that ran directly from the base of the valley to the top. I took a lot of photos I hoped would do it justice, because the scenery was outstanding.

Later I had a great talk with Ricardo about dinosaurs, the canyons we had been searching, and what they were trying to accomplish on the expeditions. He started off the conversation by bringing out a folder full of 8″ x 10″ overlapping aerial satellite photos giving a black and white view of the whole region. He showed how the areas to prospect were picked, and how other things were being done with the GPS waypoints throughout the region, in an effort to accurately map everything.

There were graduate students with us who were putting together scientific data on all kinds of things, including just plain geology. Overall, I found it educational, and I noticed the entire group was having fun together.

While riding back from Talampaya National Park, in the small truck with only three Argentinean students, I had a great time trying to communicate. Thankfully, one of them was able to speak a little English. All were under thirty and very interested in me and the project. We talked a little about the United States and a little about the Argentinean culture.

On the way back to camp that evening, those in my car chose to go through a small town to try and buy a birthday cake for a nice guy who worked at the base camp and kept it clean each day. Being a Sunday evening, we didn't have any luck buying the cake, but we bought a large white candle that would be stuck into something at supper for the birthday celebration.

I got to observe life in a small town as we stopped at the gas station and grocery store after driving up and down the narrow streets. The people all seemed friendly but kept to themselves. They seemed to have a quiet, simple lifestyle. There were various dogs roaming the streets while small children played under the trees. The homes were very close to the narrow roads and were painted in pastel colors. It was obvious the people of that town didn't have a lot of money, but they seemed to be content.

When we got back on the main road and started toward the off-road that led across the desert to our base camp, we passed a military checkpoint. We were stopped and questioned, but the driver, who spoke Spanish, handled it with ease. He had to present a driver's license. The guards looked over our vehicle carefully. They waved us through, and we arrived at camp just about dark. Shortly thereafter, I went to the campfire for what I hoped was another evening feast. I knew we wouldn't eat supper until 10:00, but I was getting used to drinking the fine Argentinean wines and enjoying conversation with the others around the open fire while the meal was being prepared. I took extra clothes and a flashlight to the campfire. Once the sun went down, the air quickly became quite cool. It was so dark after midnight, I knew I would need a flashlight to find my tent.

On Monday morning, I got up at 7:00. It was very cold. The sky was blue as the sun rose over the horizon. There were almost no clouds in the sky. Usually there was a distant haze in the air, and you weren't able to see far away. That morning, I could clearly see a long range of mountains in the distance, the upper half totally covered in snow. I was told one mountain in the middle of that range was named Fatima. It was the second tallest mountain in South America. To the opposite side, and well into the distance, could be seen other parts of the Andes Mountains. They were also covered in snow. I had read the tallest mountain in the Andes range was 21,000 feet in elevation.

Breakfast consisted of only hard bread with fruit jelly. I noticed that we were beginning to run out of the large variety of food items we had at the beginning of the trip. I found a single apple and an orange and ate those by the campfire. I filled my water containers to the top out of a big plastic barrel. I knew I would have a long day in the heat, because most of us were expected to travel back to the top of "Hearn Mountain." Oscar and Ricardo had let us know they were very excited about what we might find there.

There were three volunteers and two graduate students who decided to go in the opposite direction that day. They were going to run a heavy jack hammer and use chisels in an effort to excavate a large dinosaur lodged in hard, red rock on a hillside a few miles from camp. Oscar told us they were hoping the entire skeleton was in the hill, because they had not recovered a complete skeleton from that species of dinosaur in all their previous expeditions. Only time would tell what they would ultimately uncover, as the rock was slowly removed over many weeks.

My group reached the top of Hearn Mountain, and one of the men remarked that it was a beautiful day. The sun was beginning to warm up everything. I knew it would soon get very hot, and I took off my long sleeve shirt. The team members began to disperse in all directions. We had been told to report back to that starting GPS location at 4:30 in the afternoon.

Over the course of the day, I'm sure I walked six miles traveling up and down hills on loose soil. The heavy gear and water I was carrying in my backpack didn't make it any easier. The straps rubbed my shoulders, and I could feel they were beginning to get raw. Even though I daily powdered my feet in the morning and covered the blisters with moleskin, they still bothered me. I also noticed that my lower back became really tired during the day.

Later in the afternoon, I saw a black vulture, a soaring Andean condor and another small flock of squawking green and purple parrots. Two of the parrots flew very low and were not ten feet above my head as they passed. They were beautiful with deep iridescent colors that glistened in the sunlight.

We found many new dinosaur bones that day. Oscar told us he continued to be pleased with the site, but most of the volunteers began to express their feelings about being exhausted after making the long climb each day. One of them asked me how I ever found the place. I told him I had been foolish to have wandered so far while prospecting without anyone at the camp knowing where I was.

As I walked around looking at the ground, I occasionally would walk upon a site that someone else had just discovered. It would be marked with a piece of white toilet paper stuck under the edge of a rock. Those sites were all interesting to me. Some contained large bones and others contained fragments of bone that had eroded on the surface or had washed down the hill.

One spot I noticed, where Ricardo was busy digging around a group of bones, was spectacular. As I walked up to see his progress, I saw five large vertebras in a line with part of a scapula protruding from the ground. There were large rocks nearby that contained embedded rows of scutes from that particular dinosaur. Scutes had been described to me as bony, armored plates that ran parallel to the backbone in rows, separated by a narrow space in between each one.

A little farther around a ridge, I noticed Oscar digging in a creek bed. His find was a large femur bone three feet long. There was also part of a pelvis bone beside it from a very large dinosaur.

As I passed other volunteers walking and crisscrossing each other, they would tell me about their finds. Everyone was excited, and the best way I could describe it was that it was like a big Easter egg hunt, except we were finding the remains of animals that had lived and died over two hundred million years ago. I couldn't help but think about how unique each of the finds really was. I hoped many of them would eventually get fully excavated and transferred to the museum in San Juan.

On Tuesday, the sky began to get light at 6:40. The air remained still and very cold. During the night, I had slept in my snug "mummy" sleeping bag. I had kept my tent zipped tight in order to stay comfortable and knock off the cold breeze that rippled the tent constantly during the night.

After wiping my face with a wet cloth and brushing my teeth at a big washbasin, I made sure I filled my water containers for the day. We were down to only a single barrel of water. I was told one of the guys planned to take a truck on a three hour drive that afternoon to buy some more for the last few days. By volume, the water we were using cost about the same as wine. I thought that was unusual.

Breakfast was again only hard bread with fruit jelly and a slice of cheese. I saved a small amount of sliced ham and added it to some cheese and made two sandwiches to take with me for lunch.

As I sat and waited for everyone, I thought back about the night before as we had gathered around the campfire. I had looked up in the night sky, and remembered thinking I had never seen a sky so full of stars. It was probably because there were no towns anywhere close casting lights upward into the darkness. That night's meal had been really good. It was hard to know what the other guys put into the big black pot that boiled each night over the campfire, but there seemed to always be plenty of cut up vegetables, some form of noodles, a little meat and tomato sauce. It might have been because I was getting so much exercise each day, but the food was generally so good each night I had been having two helpings. Of course, there was no shortage of wine to go with the food, and it topped off the evening.

I had been counting the number of people at camp each night. There were nineteen, five of those being Argentinean graduate students. Before coming on the trip, I had read there would be only six volunteers and two scientists, but there were actually nine volunteers, two scientists, one older fellow who just took care of the campsite, the graduate students and a few museum workers who came along to help out. Everyone got along very well, and there always seemed to be a lot of laughing and stories told about the day's experiences around the campfire each night.

As I sat there waiting to start the day, I realized my feet and legs were really tired. I made the decision not to prospect on the top of the mountain with the group. I figured that a day's rest would also help my lower back pain. Instead, I chose to do something entirely different and go with the other team of workers who had been excavating each day on a hillside about two miles away from the base camp. They got there by riding in one of the trucks. That site was the one where the dinosaur was originally found in a small hillside embedded in hard sediment.

In spite of my earlier desire to take a day of rest, I ended up helping operate a jackhammer that ran off a gas powered generator. The generator was hand carried to the site by three of us after getting the truck as close as possible. Seven of us took turns using the jackhammer to bust up the sediment into small pieces. The work progressed very slowly. When I was not using the larger power hammer, I was using a heavy metal hammer with a bulky, wooden handle and a large chisel. My hands and arms tired quickly, and I had to take frequent breaks. The sun got increasingly hotter as the day progressed. There were no clouds in the sky. I was really glad when we finally took a lunch break under a big shaded overhang.

The bones of the dinosaur we were excavating were a beautiful, greenish-blue color locked tightly within the red rock. Many of the bones throughout the area took on a variety of colors depending on the particular sediment and minerals that had surrounded them when they were originally covered millions of years earlier. We had found many that were mostly gray, but others had taken on a slight bluish-white cast. The greenish-blue ones we were excavating that day really stood out.

As it turned out, where I had intended to take a day of rest, I ended up having one of the most exhausting days yet. As we finished and rode back to the campsite in the truck, I decided the next day I would go back to the mountain top to do more prospecting, if we were not assigned something different.

When everyone started showing up at the campfire that evening, there were stories of good finds the group had made during the day at the top of the mountain. Oscar and Ricardo kidded me about having found the place that was so exhausting to reach.

At the same time, they agreed it was a wonderful spot. They were happy with the quantity and quality of what had been found there so far. They told me they had plans to take Team Three, the last team of the season, there each day during the final two weeks. Maybe that team would be able to completely excavate and enclose in plaster some of the best finds our team had made. I knew it would definitely be a lot of hard work to get the larger plaster casts off the mountain and back down to base camp.

The next day started off very cold again. As everyone sat around the campfire and finished eating breakfast, we waited for Oscar and Ricardo to arrive and tell us what they had in store for us. When they arrived, Oscar said that instead of going back to the top of the mountain, we would all climb aboard the two four-wheel drive vehicles and drive to a place they had picked out from aerial photos.

We loaded up and bumped along through gullies for an hour until we reached a small dirt road. We then traveled an additional hour for a total of 75 miles. The trucks were pulled off the road near the foothills of a mountain range. Nearby, a fellow came out of a one-roomed house with a mud-covered floor followed by a small dog. The structure was made of sticks with gravel spread on the roof. He wanted to know what we were doing in the area.

Oscar approached him and spoke in Spanish. He told him we were on a scientific expedition and needed a place to park the trucks for a few hours. The old fellow was very nice and told us we were welcome to park the vehicles near his house. He even offered advice on the layout of the foothills and where we should start looking for dinosaur bones.

Fifteen of us spread out, walking in all directions, after being told to be back at the trucks at 3:00. The original destination I picked out was a mountain range I could see a mile in the distance. I set a waypoint on my GPS where the trucks were parked, so I would be able to find them later in the day. Once I arrived at the edge of that mountain range, I went up and down the lower hillsides and later walked through a large valley covered by gray and white mounds with no success.

Off in the distance was a mountain with red sediment layers running left to right. I figured I could reach it in thirty minutes. As I arrived and began to walk up and down its ridges, I looked across the open plains behind me and saw a large sand storm gaining in intensity and approaching rapidly. At that time, the visibility where I was standing was good with a clear sky, but the storm a mile away looked like a thick fog coming through the valley between two mountain ranges.

It instantly scared me. I had heard others tell stories of getting caught in a Zonda, where they could not see because of the fiercely blowing sand and dust that had started for no obvious reason. I was at least a mile and a half from where we had been let off the trucks. I knew I had a GPS waypoint set on my hand-held navigation device. I looked out across the area I needed to cross and realized there were drop-offs, as well as many thorn bushes I needed to avoid. I also realized that so far I had not been required to use the GPS without the ability to see other landmarks. So being afraid, I started walking very fast while I could still see.

As the sand storm caught up to me, the wind hit like a sand blaster. The temperature increased instantly by about ten degrees. I could see a little between the hard gusts and used that opportunity to move forward, while looking for canyon drop-offs and avoiding the dangerous thorn bushes that were scattered everywhere.

It took me close to two hours to get back to the truck. I was certainly relieved to be there. Others started drifting in from the field, and finally all were accounted for nearly an hour later. A few had found a small cave type overhang and had stayed there hoping for the sand storm to let up. In the arid desert of Argentina, I had heard the temperature and wind could change dramatically in a very short period of time, and on that afternoon I experienced it firsthand. Oscar told us later that during the summer months he had seen the temperature change from 110 degrees to about 40 degrees in less than an hour when a big weather front moved through suddenly.

Because we had left the field an hour early due to the Zonda and everyone was hot, we decided to stop by a small gas station to get a beer and cool off. One drink led to two and then three, etc. Before we left, most everyone was drunk.

On the way back to base camp there was a lot of singing, both in English and Spanish. The Argentinean driving our truck was having a good time and decided to drive fast through the ruts and gullies. The last quarter of a mile was flat red sand, but the tire tracks we made with the truck wove back and forth around the thorn bushes and other vegetation. He fishtailed around the turns while driving much too fast. I didn't know if we would make it back to camp alive. When we slid to a halt at the campsite, the truck's occupants exploded in cheers. The entire group was really drunk and glad to be back.

I learned that one of the guys had driven to a remote village and purchased some additional meat. Supper was not scheduled until around 10:00, as usual. There were large slabs of ribs and other cuts of beef roasted over hot coals. Along with the meat, we had potatoes, bread and all the wine we could drink. I slept well that night.

On Thursday morning, the wind was still blowing, and it was much colder. I could hardly stand to go to the washbasin and clean my face. I was shivering. After a simple breakfast, we discussed what we would do for our last day of prospecting. Everyone knew we would break up camp and leave early to travel all day back to San Juan the next morning. We were hoping to make some good discoveries on our last day.

We were given different options. Some chose to drive a few miles away to pick up the plaster casts scattered around the area that contained some of the better finds of the last two weeks. I chose to climb to the top of the mountain one last time and explore a few new areas with Lou, Oscar and Ricardo. I also wanted to photograph some of the things that had been found on the day I had gone to the other location and ran the jackhammer.

When our small crew reached the top, I stopped to see a large find of bones Ricardo had been excavating at the edge of a steep cliff. The exposed leg bones, vertebras and pelvic bones quickly made it obvious it had been a large dinosaur. I took some photographs, and then Lou and I went off on our own. We walked over a mile along the edge of the cliff. We were trying to follow a particular layer of sediment that had given us some wonderful bones over the last week.

I ended up discovering two large vertebras six inches in diameter on a hillside and then found many other assorted bones fifty yards away. At a different spot, I found one leg bone that was three feet long and eight inches wide at the large knobs on the end. It must have been a large dinosaur. After Oscar saw it, he told me the species, from 210 million years ago, had been about twenty feet long, including the tail.

After hours of walking up and down hills, we decided to call it a day and return to camp. We did a little more prospecting on the way back. It took us more than two hours to cover roughly two and a half miles of very bad terrain. When we arrived back at camp, Lou and I met with Oscar and Ricardo and gave them the coordinates from our GPS for our best finds. That way, Team Three would have something to work on after they arrived.

Later on that evening, I walked into the main tent where Oscar and Ricardo were working with a laptop computer. On the table in front of them were pieces of a small skull and pieces of a small skeleton. The skull was only three inches long and had a row of small teeth hanging out on one side. Ricardo explained it had been found in the Los Colorados Formation during the 2003 season. They were busy, as I walked into the tent, writing a scientific paper on that find. They described it to me as one of the very first vertebrates that had ever walked the earth and later evolved into what we know today as the modern day crocodile. It was tiny, but I could see the resemblance.

I sat down and thought about all the fun I had enjoyed over the last two weeks, and everything that I had learned. My feet were sore from blisters, and my skin was dirt red from not being able to bathe. I decided it was time to start packing up everything in my tent. That way, I would be ready to leave camp the next morning at 9:00. As I sat there, I remembered I was scheduled to fly out of San Juan Monday morning, four days in the future, so I still had more adventure ahead.

On Friday morning, we were hoping the long trip back to San Juan would be somewhat uneventful. We had all gotten up early and eaten, packed our belongings, and were ready to leave on time. The sun was bright and the sky was blue. Gone was the Zonda with its hot blowing winds and the otherwise harsh cold weather. It was actually a nice day.

We had ten minutes to take a group photo. Oscar promised to send the photo to each of us by email sometime in the near future. I left my tent as I had set it up two weeks earlier, with permission from Oscar. I knew it could be used not only the rest of the season, but also during the next year's expeditions. In truth, it was so covered with a thick red film of dirt, both inside and out, that I didn't really want to pack it. I knew I needed the extra space in my duffle bag for items I had purchased on the trip.

The drive to San Juan took seven hours. I was able to get a seat by an open window so I wouldn't have trouble with carsickness on the winding road. We stopped midway for a gasoline break. I used my time to walk around the small village and observe the people, houses and obvious lifestyles. Again, everyone was friendly. Gentle dogs and small children roamed the streets.

I purchased a bag full of small wrapped candies in a market and went into the street. I gave the whole bag to the first child who came up to me. Instantly, the other children converged on the goodies, and they were shared freely.

Arriving back at the Hotel Alkazar was a pleasure. All I could think of was to get to my room and take a bath. It had been over two weeks since my last shower or bath, and I needed one badly. Normally I took a shower, but I felt it was time to take a nice, warm, long bath. After soaking and scrubbing for what seemed like an hour, I dried off on the white towels. I noticed there was still red coming off my body and onto the towels. When I got out of the tub, it had a ring of red around the upper edge that I couldn't rub off. I figured it would take a few more baths and showers before the red color on my body would eventually be gone.

Saturday morning was spent mostly in the lobby saying good-bye to everyone. Some were taking the bus a hundred miles south to Mendosa to catch a plane, and others were taking the cab to the San Juan airport. A few had made arrangements to stay the next night in Buenos Aires and attend a night club to view real Argentina tango dancing. For me, I was scheduled to remain in San Juan until early Monday, when I would start the long voyage back to Wilmington, North Carolina.

Later, I spent a few hours walking around the city by myself. I stopped at a street café to eat lunch. A well done hamburger with fries and a Quilmes beer tasted very good while I watched people come and go on the streets. Most of the retail businesses were closed from noon to four o'clock. That gave me time to kill in a central park under a shady tree, until I could do a little shopping later in the day.

When I noticed some of the stores beginning to open, I walked up and down the carefully laid out city until I found a small shop with quality leather products that had been made in Argentina. As was the food, those items were about half what the cost would have been in the United States.

After purchasing a few things, I returned to the Alkazar Hotel somewhere around seven o'clock, just in time to meet a few of the incoming team members from Team Three. When they found out I had been part of Team Two, they asked many questions. I had decided ahead of time I would only tell them that they were about to experience "a big adventure."

I found that statement was not enough for them, so I gave in and revealed some of the things we had experienced over the last two weeks. I could tell by the looks on their faces, it was more than they expected. When I asked how many had brought GPS locators, which was recommended in the literature sent to each of us before the trip, the response was negative from all of them. I was sure they would be sorry because I knew my GPS had been very valuable and might have saved my life during the Zonda. I had used it constantly to mark fossils and waypoints, so I could find my way back to the trucks each day. I realized that having it with me had given me a constant peace of mind.

Oscar came by the Hotel Alkazar at 9:00 that night, as planned, for a short orientation and then left. He explained that he was busy getting everything ready for travel back out early the next morning.

I went to eat supper with the new group, and by the time we got back to the hotel it was after 1:00 in the morning. I quickly said good-bye to Team Three and went to bed. I knew they would have to be up, checked out and ready to go at 7:00 the next morning. I wished them all a good trip. They were exactly where I had been a little over two weeks earlier. I had surely learned a lot in that short time and was thankful to have returned safely.

*"Your living is determined not so much
by what life brings to you
as by the attitude you bring to life; not so much
by what happens to you as by the way
your mind looks at what happens."*

Khalil Gibran

South Africa
August 2010

On Wednesday afternoon, August 4th, I left the Wilmington airport and flew to Atlanta. There I met my younger brother, Jim. David Keith, the owner of Gray Ghost Safaris, and another hunter, Robbie, were there also. We were on our way to South Africa for an exciting safari hunt for various African animals.

The long 17 hour flight from Atlanta took us over the Atlantic Ocean directly to Johannesburg, South Africa. It was the second leg of a three plane trip for me. I knew it would be a long time to sit in a small coach seat, but it was the least expensive way to travel. Our plans were to later arrive in Port Elizabeth, after one additional flight. There was a six hour time change between my home and that part of Africa.

For months I had been looking forward to experiencing the southern part of Africa with my brother. We didn't get to spend much time together anymore, and on this trip we were scheduled to be together for almost two weeks. When we had talked about the trip earlier, he let me know he was planning to harvest a few unusual animals that he could have mounted and hung in his large home in Brentwood, Tennessee. We talked about specific species he might want to bring back. He said he would make the decision on the spot, depending on what animals we encountered. I knew he was definitely interested in animals with beautiful fur coloring and long, twisted horns that weren't normally seen in North America. The only African animal like that, whose name I knew before the trip, was the kudu. It was a very large animal with three foot long horns. I felt sure it would make a beautiful head and shoulder mount if he could manage to harvest one during the hunt.

I spent most of the day before leaving home trying to put together the critical items I would need for the trip. One of those items was a camera I had recently purchased with an 18X zoom telephoto lens. It had a video capability with three memory chips of 8 gigs each, so I could capture much of the action at prime times during the hunt. I thought the camera would work well for my photos. Jim told me he was bringing a very nice Nikon camera with a special telephoto lens.

Early on I couldn't decide what I felt about being a part of a safari hunt where animals would be hunted and killed for trophies. I knew there were people who didn't feel good about hunting, and I had heard many different opinions, both pro and con. Some of the serious hunters viewed it as a form of strengthening the herd by removing older animals near the end of their lives. Others had strong feelings that nothing should be killed. Those people took offense at any type of hunting. I decided that I was somewhere in the middle of those two ways of thinking. My main goal was to spend time with my younger brother while he hunted. I also wanted to see the unusual animals of Africa in their natural habitat, take photos and just enjoy the trip. I was considered a "tag along" by Gray Ghosts Safaris because I would not be hunting. Therefore, my cost was less than everyone else's. I would only be taking photographs and documenting everything in a daily journal.

When I was younger, I hunted with my two brothers and my dad while I was still in high school. We shot rabbits, doves, quail and an occasional fox. After one of those hunts, I felt bad about the animals we had killed. The last time I participated in a hunting trip was at the age of twenty-five. Somewhere after that time, I lost interest. Otherwise I fished, which was a big part of my life, and sometimes I felt bad about killing and eating the fish. With the animals we would shoot on our African trip, I had been told the meat would be saved in a freezer and eventually sold and eaten by people throughout the southern part of Africa.

The land we would be hunting was part of a personally owned game farm, and the animals roamed freely on approximately 35 square miles or 25,000 acres. Some of the land was open and bare, with only a few trees or clumps of bushes, but much of it was heavily covered with thick vegetation. Each kill would involve a real hunt and a challenge. Knowing that, I knew I would enjoy being involved in the search for a large variety of African game animals with Jim.

The flight to Port Elizabeth from Johannesburg lasted two hours. I had spent the whole time in the air talking to two individuals who sat on either side of me. They had strange accents that sounded British or Australian, and I felt sure I sounded odd and different to them.

In Port Elizabeth we were met by the owner of the lodge where we would be staying for the next 10 days. His name was Keith Gradwell. He told us that we still had more than three hours to travel northeast in his four-wheel drive truck to get to our final destination. It was 9:30 at night, and we were all exhausted as we boarded his truck. For our long ride, there were two people in the front seats plus Jim, Robbie and me tightly cramped in the back with no leg room. We were all lying on top of each other and very uncomfortable. The luggage and guns had been stacked in the back behind us.

After an eventful ride through the dark, where we saw strange animals on the sides of the road looking into our headlights, we drove onto Keith's property and game farm named "Woodlands." He verified what I had been told earlier, that the property included over 25,000 acres of land, with a large stone lodge standing near the center. He told us he had moved there in 1963 with his parents, and they had purchased additional land over the years so as to turn it into a large game farm. Originally, his parents had farmed goats on the property. We were so wired upon arriving at the lodge, we stayed up talking until after 1:30 before finally going to bed.

Everyone had decided to get up at 6:30 the next morning. We needed to go out and sight-in the rifles with scopes at a firing range set up a few miles from the lodge. That time arrived much too quickly. I got up, took a shower, shaved and ate breakfast while containing my excitement about our upcoming adventure. Everyone but me fired the rifles at a small target 25 yards away and then at the same target 100 yards away. After feeling comfortable their guns had fired accurately, we were on our way for our first morning of hunting.

We drove through rocky, dusty roads while going up and down hills. We reached an area where we could get out and walk on flat land which was covered by many thorn bushes. Everyone had binoculars with them, and mine turned out to be better than I had expected when I had purchased them. I quickly discovered that having a good pair of binoculars was an important part of the hunt. Throughout the day, we spent many hours looking through them for game animals in the hillsides and valleys.

The first animal we hoped to find was a kudu. It's similar to an American elk, with large spiraling horns twisting upward into points approximately 30 to 36 inches from the top of its head. It's covered with white, brown, tan and faint black colors forming distinct patterns on its body and head.

Off in the distance, we heard a baboon in the top of a tree. It barked like a dog to alert the other animals that we were coming. Baboons spook very easily since they have such good eyesight, and it was gone in an instant into the dense vegetation as we approached within its safe zone.

After standing on a wooded hilltop and observing other hillsides across an open valley, Rob Zanoncelli, our personal hunter, spotted a male kudu standing in a thickly wooded area approximately 300 yards away. It was our first sighting of one of the animals we were interested in harvesting. It was beautiful. The kudu was facing the sun so we were able, by using the binoculars, to see it fairly well. Rob told us that kudu was not fully mature, but it sure looked large to Jim and me. He told us he would only allow Jim to shoot a fully mature, trophy-size animal. The younger ones were off limits. As we waited hoping other kudus would appear, we saw warthogs in the distance scurrying around in the dust with their babies. From the hilltop, I could see for three-fourths of a mile across the rolling land.

We stood at that one spot for about thirty minutes, and the immature kudu at 300 yards never flinched. He watched our every move. I wondered how many other eyes were observing us from behind green trees and thick bushes.

Finally, we moved on and searched other favorable areas, always with the binoculars. My arms and lower back began to tire and ache from constantly holding them to my eyes. Tami, a black African helper who was assigned to us, carried a five foot cane tripod that was roughly held together with tape and cord. After setting it up, he rested his binoculars on top as he searched the hillsides and valleys. I decided I would get something like that for myself. I found out that Tami also carried the tripod so Jim would have a brace in which to rest his rifle when the time came to take a shot. It helped him steady the scope's crosshairs for a perfect shot from a great distance.

We gave up after a short stop at another spot and drove back to the lodge so we could eat lunch and rest a while. I was glad, because I was still really tired from the traveling to South Africa and the short five hours of sleep I had after arriving.

At the lodge after lunch, we sat on the back deck and looked across the open savannah surrounding us while Robbie told us about shooting a zebra that morning. He had been assigned a different personal hunter and had gone out in a separate truck for his hunt. He described the zebra as a beautiful animal. While we had been eating lunch, four helpers who normally served as skinners had gone out in a pickup truck to bring the zebra back. It arrived just as Jim and I were about to board our truck for the afternoon hunt. As we passed the zebra, I had Rob stop our vehicle. I jumped out and quickly took some photos. Later that afternoon it was skinned, so the hide could be tanned to make a zebra skin rug. The meat was kept in a large freezer on the property. It would later be sold to a dealer who would distribute it to the local people.

Jim, Rob, Tami and I spent the afternoon hours searching from hilltops while looking through binoculars. By that time, I had my own makeshift tripod on which I rested my arms, and it helped tremendously. We spotted small herds of different African animals in the distance. I slowly learned their names as they were repeated over and over to me by our guide. All of them seemed to have horns of different shapes and interesting colors of fur. After three hours, we spotted a group of giraffes one-half mile away, along with a small herd of elands, followed by some impalas. The elands were beautiful, and we were told that both the male and females had horns. The older bulls were supposed to be heavier and had much thicker horns. There were no bulls in that group of elands, so we focused on the impalas that were beautifully colored.

We quietly boarded our vehicle and drove down a hillside as we approached the impalas behind a thicket of trees. We got out and slowly advanced closer and closer by foot with Jim's rifle ready. Before long we were within 350 yards, and we noticed there were ten impalas in the group following the female elands up a hillside. It was late in the afternoon, and the sun was going down quickly. The shadows from trees and bushes had begun to lengthen. We moved from one large bush to the next over loose stones and rocks that were everywhere. The goal was to see if we could get close enough to get a good shot at the large male impala leading the group. We finally got within range at 6:20, just fifteen minutes before it was totally dark.

Jim and Rob moved ahead so as to set up the shot. The impala herd moved restlessly in the distance up the hillside. We tried to close in on them before they spooked. The breeze was blowing into our faces, and that was perfect because our scents were moving away from the animals. Tami moved forward with the bamboo tripod, and Rob helped Jim with placement so he could make an attempt at a shot. As I watched from a short distance, I wondered if Jim could see clearly through his rifle's scope because of the lack of light. Rob had brought his small hunting dog, a Jack Russell terrier named Casey. He used it to help track game through the thick bush, but only if the game had been injured by a gun shot. The dog remained very quiet and just watched intently without making a sound. That really surprised me, because all of the Jack Russell terriers I had known were quite active and constantly jumped up and down while barking for no apparent reason.

Rob told Jim it was time to take a shot. As he took aim, I readied myself for the loud noise the rifle would soon make. As we waited, the entire impala herd continued to move around the hillside and restlessly weaved around bushes. I was sure at any moment they would spook and disappear quickly over the nearest hill. Jim got ready to shoot more than once as the impalas kept crossing each other. Finally, the leader, the largest and oldest in the herd, stood sideways at 180 yards. Rob whispered to Jim that it was time to take the shot. His gun exploded very loudly as I saw the impala immediately hit the ground. The rest of the herd disappeared in a heartbeat over the nearest ridge.

As we walked the 180 yards toward the fallen animal, I noticed how quickly it was getting dark. Rob told Tami to go back through the bush and bring the truck to our location so we could load the impala. I took some photographs with my flash attachment hooked on the camera, while Jim and Rob talked about the hunt and the earlier action. Jim was very excited. Looking at the dead animal, I saw that its colors were beautiful, and the long 19 inch mature horns were perfect and undamaged.

As Tami arrived at the spot with his headlights on, I noticed it was completely dark. Rob and Tami loaded the animal for our

ride back to the camp. We talked about the hunt the entire time
we rode back. At the lodge, in front of the vehicle's headlights,
we took a variety of photographs using both my and Jim's cameras. The plan was to instruct the skinners to prepare the impala
so the skin could either be used as a full mount or just a head
and shoulder mount. We knew the final decision could be decided later on between Jim and his taxidermist back in the United
States.

At the lodge that night, we sat around the warm fireplace and
discussed our adventures of the day. I got out my small bottle
of Crown Royal bourbon whiskey I had brought from home. I
poured a small amount of it over ice and added a bit of coke. It
sure tasted good, and it relaxed me. Supper included pork chops,
potatoes and peas along with a green salad, apple pie and carrot
cake. It was very tasty and appreciated after our long tiring day.
After resting for a brief period by the fire, we retired for the night
at 9:30. The plan was to get up at 6:00 the following morning, so
we could leave the lodge by 7:00.

Saturday morning started with a nice breakfast of cereal, milk,
yogurt, toast, jelly and a banana. By 7:00 we were in the truck
and on our way. For the first two hours we drove over bumpy,
dusty roads filled with large stones. Rob sighted a large male
warthog one-quarter of a mile away near a hilltop. The warthog
was surrounded by small shrubs and thorn bushes. Rob, Jim,
Tami and I exited the truck and walked carefully in that direction. We slowed as we got close and searched the area for the
animal. Soon it was sighted again. Jim set up the bamboo tripod
so he could take a shot with his rifle. Casey, the Jack Russell
terrier, was with us and ready to go. We had laughed earlier
at how aggressive that little white and brown dog was during a
hunt. He was perfectly quiet until he heard the gunshot and then
went absolutely nuts to get to the animal.

As Jim readied for the shot, I saw the nervous anticipation
on the little dog's face. He watched Jim chamber the shell in

his single shot, bolt action rifle and steady it on the tripod. In Africa they do not allow a hunter to carry an automatic weapon, and a single shot, bolt action rifle was the only option. When the shot was fired, the dog went wild to get to the warthog, but Rob snatched him up by his harness so the warthog would not kill him before it died. The shot didn't immediately kill the animal, and Jim had to shoot a second shot before it finally settled quietly to the ground. We approached the warthog carefully to make sure it was dead, and then Rob let Casey loose. The little dog began biting the downed animal. He started lapping up the red blood in a pool on the ground. Then he climbed on the warthog and started eating at the bloody opening on its side. He proved to be a little wild man at the site of a kill, and became invaluable in tracking wounded animals. Rob told Tami to go back and bring the truck alongside so the pig could be loaded. I took a bunch of photos, as Jim and Rob discussed what had just occurred.

After we positioned the animal, and I had taken another series of photos, it was finally loaded into the vehicle. It was interesting how ugly the warthog's face was with large, natural bumps on its head. Its body looked similar to a pig, but the head was strange and elongated with large, curved, white tusks sticking out the sides of its mouth on both the upper and lower jaws. The tusks looked like white ivory, were curved upward to a point and were approximately nine inches long. I decided I would not like an angry warthog to tear into me.

The warthog incident occurred at 8:00 in the morning, so we had time to focus our hunt on a kudu and an oryx, also known as a gemsbok. Both of those animals were beautiful creatures with extremely long horns, distinct patterns and varied fur colors. While sitting on a mountain ridge, we glassed (the term used for looking through binoculars during a hunt) for a good hour trying to pick up the sight of a large male kudu. We were only able to find immature males. That was not what Rob wanted us to harvest. I thought the ones we saw, in and around the bushes and small trees a quarter of a mile away, were fully mature adults, because the horns and bodies were large. But they were not, according to Rob. He explained that a full adult's horns faced the front at the very top points. The ones we had been seeing had tips that twisted and faced toward the back.

At noon, as we headed back toward the lodge, we saw off in the distance herds of impalas, four zebras, many red hartebeests, more warthogs and a host of other animals. On a hilltop, four large giraffes stood to our left. By using the binoculars, I could see their skin patterns and colors in the sun. They were beautiful animals. No one from our group would consider shooting one of those.

When we arrived back at the lodge, the four helpers were already skinning the kills of the hunters from the other two vehicles. There was a male red hartebeest with reddish fur and a head similar to a horse with short, twisted black horns that angled off to the back. That animal probably weighed 250 pounds and was quite odd looking. There was a warthog with large ivory colored tusks and another horned animal with a white face. I later learned it was called a blesbok. I looked in a shed close by and noticed a bunch of skins that were drying and being made ready for tanning with eventual shipment back to the United States for taxidermy work. I didn't know what the system was for keeping up with the skins and horns shot by the different hunters. I later learned it involved attaching small labeled tags with wires to them before they were stored.

The wind picked up in the morning, so we waited in the lodge after lunch until 2:00 to go back out for the afternoon hunt. We would still be looking for a nice mature kudu.

Jim began to work on setting up a separate hunt for a lynx, a type of small cat similar to an American bobcat but larger. That hunt would use dogs that chased and treed the lynx after picking up its scent. That would not take place for a few more days and would be at an entirely different location. We would find out more about the details after Keith called a friend who owned a large sheep farm. His friend was having problems with lynx killing his sheep.

At 2:00, after a nice lunch and a short time to relax, we continued our hunt. We drove a few miles until we reached an open stretch of land broken only by a huge number of brown termite mounds that seemed to be everywhere. Each mound was three feet in diameter and one to two feet tall. Many of the mounds had been invaded during the night by aardvarks, a nocturnal mammal. They dug a round hole in the side of the mound to get to the termites that they ate. After the aardvarks were finished, the hard termite mound looked a little like a small dog house with a round dark entry hole at ground level. As I looked out over the flat African plain, there must have been thousands of those termite mounds, along with an occasional small green tree or bush.

We stopped the vehicle and noticed a half mile in the distance a herd of black wildebeests feeding and roaming loosely. By looking through the binoculars, we also saw small groupings of springboks that were smaller deerlike mammals with beautiful reddish-brown, tan, white and black markings. The males had horns that were 10" to 12" long.

On Rob's advice, Jim and I positioned ourselves beside one of the isolated green bushes in the middle of that vast, open land. Rob decided to stay with us while Tami drove the four wheel drive across the open savannah in an effort to turn the herd of wildebeests and springboks toward us. As he left to try to accomplish that, we settled in and readied ourselves for what was to come. Tami drove slowly around the brown termite mounds and disappeared into the distance behind small ridges and depressions in the otherwise flat land. He was probably gone for an hour before we noticed a small group of springboks headed our way over a slight hill. I moved farther around behind the large bush we were using for cover. The springboks continued in our direction, and soon three of them were close enough for Jim to get a shot. Rob checked through his binoculars and picked out the best and oldest male with the nicest horns. Jim slowly positioned his rifle with the powerful scope on the bamboo tripod and soon there was a shot echoing loudly. The front male went down quickly. That shot was made from approximately 150 yards.

We walked over and checked the springbok that had died instantly. The beautifully marked animal was later loaded in the back of the vehicle when Tami returned. That happened around 4:00 in the afternoon. We decided we might still have time to hunt for one of the big bulls from the black wildebeest herd, since they were still in the area.

We again settled near a single green bush in the middle of the open land. We had moved a quarter of a mile from the first bush we had earlier hidden behind. The thinking was that the animals probably would now associate danger with the area where we had first started hunting. Tami again left in the truck, while I lay on the ground and waited. Rob, Jim and I talked, told stories and jokes, as we waited for the wildebeest herd to move in our direction.

Somewhere around 5:00, we noticed black dots on the horizon heading our way. The wildebeests were coming fast and passed us on the left in a mad dash. Those animals appeared to be the size of small buffalos. They were running very fast and kicking up a trail of light brown dust. The first few that passed us were females. There were probably thirty or so in a tight cluster. We waited ten minutes, and Rob noticed three large mature bulls heading toward us that had separated from the large group of females. I continued to stay hidden on the very backside of the bush, but Jim and Rob positioned themselves for a possible shot from the other side.

The three males picked up speed as they approached within 250 yards. Then suddenly, they stopped on a slight rise. As they stood and looked our way, Rob picked out the biggest one using his glassing skills and told Jim to shoot the middle bull. I held my hands over my ears, because I knew the noise would be loud. Soon the explosion occurred, and the animal was hit. It immediately ran off with the other two, but after 200 yards went down to the ground. We walked slowly in that direction and found the bull quietly laying there. Its horns were dark, perfectly formed and heavy at the base. Rob confirmed it was an old animal. He said it was probably ten years old and near the end of its life.

I took some photographs while Jim and Rob talked. Soon Tami arrived, and we loaded the very heavy, black male wildebeest into the back of the truck alongside the springbok. It was a full load. We packed all our gear in the front and drove across the openness as the sun neared the horizon. I knew within 30 minutes it would be dark because that occurred before 6:30.

On the way back toward the lodge, we passed a large herd of three to four hundred blesboks. Those were large horned mammals, almost the size of the black wildebeest, but with completely white faces surrounded by reddish-brown coloring on their heads and bodies. A mature male had slightly curved horns measuring approximately 17" long. We decided to try and hunt one of those big males the next day.

We were tired and ready for supper, which was being prepared at the lodge by a small group of black women who were very good cooks. After a little whiskey and wine, we all shared stories of the day around a large table while eating lasagna and salad followed by carrot cake. The meal was very satisfying after a long, tiring day in the sun and wind. I went to bed by 9:30, so I would be rested for our next adventure starting early the next morning.

On Sunday we did a lot of walking up and down hills that were thickly wooded and hard to move through because of the dense vegetation. We went in search of, in addition to others, the beautiful kudu and the oryx. Rob took us to a hilltop where we searched through our binoculars across to the other side of a densely covered area beyond a deep valley. We glassed for thirty minutes and then moved slowly through the brush, trees and vines down the hill, so we could be closer to the opposite side.

We stopped midway down the hill. I spotted a large kudu about 300 yards away on a hilltop. As Jim set up the tripod to steady his rifle, I thought he was planning to take a shot at the kudu, but he proceeded to shoot at an oryx which Rob had spotted down in the valley. I hadn't even seen it from where I was standing. I knew the oryx was an incredibly striking animal, with varied patterns on its fur and straight black horns almost three feet long. Jim's shot was made in a strong wind. We started down the hillside to see if he had hit the animal, because as soon as the shot was fired the animal had ducked into the undergrowth and disappeared.

Twenty minutes later, we searched a small clearing and decided that Jim had missed the animal. There was no blood anywhere to be found. Just in case, four of us searched the thick underbrush for close to an hour before exiting the woods near a small dirt road. Tami had gone back up the hill to get the truck and had driven it around to pick us up. I was glad, because I was tired and hot. My legs were sore from descending the steep hillside while stepping carefully over numerous stones of varying sizes that seemed to be everywhere. Being careful not to sprain an ankle was important.

Jim talked about how sore his Achilles tendon had gotten. He had gone through a radical operation in December to remove a bone spur from the back of his heel. The tender reattached tendon had not totally recovered. His foot and ankle swelled at the end of each day when he removed his heavy boots. He would have to lie for a while with his foot in an elevated position to let it recover.

After the oryx experience, we drove a few miles to help find a male waterbuck that had been shot that morning by David. He was the owner of Gray Ghost Safaris. He had called by cell phone and asked if we would bring Casey, who had proven to be an excellent tracker. When we arrived at the area, Casey took about thirty minutes to pick up the scent. Then he worked his way through the underbrush and located the dead waterbuck in a thicket. Casey began barking loudly before any of us could reach the spot.

When I worked myself close enough to see the fallen animal, I was surprised by its beauty and its long, perfectly curved horns. It was much larger than I had been led to believe from one of the other hunters. We later left the area while four men, who had been called to the spot by cell phone, prepared to remove the waterbuck and take it back to the lodge to be skinned.

Lunch was to be a special event that day. We were told we would enjoy a picnic, set up by the ladies, in a clearing under some thick shade trees in the middle of the woods, instead of at the big table in the lodge. When we arrived at the site, the women had already put out the food, drinks, fold-up chairs and all the accessories. Everything was ready for us. It was obvious they had been working hard cooking our lunch over a burning campfire. All we had to do was to walk into the shaded area, sit down and eat roasted chicken, orange squash and salad with homemade bread. It was wonderful, and a great idea for a different way to experience our meal.

After cleaning up the makeshift picnic area in the woods, we left for the afternoon hunt at 3:00. By that time it was beginning to turn quite cold. There was an approaching weather front made obvious by a band of dark clouds hanging over the mountain tops and the wind blowing more than normal. We wanted to find one of the elusive kudus, but the conditions were not cooperating.

We spent the next couple of hours searching the hilltops for game, but only got close enough for a long shot at a small animal called a mountain reedbok. That animal was very fast, easily spooked, and the males would not stand in one place for very long. Jim and Rob tracked the little animal for most of an hour over the hilltops and through the fields. Jim finally set up the tripod and took a long shot into the wind from 250 yards. The bullet hit the dirt beside the little critter. It exited quickly just as the sun was beginning to set in the sky.

We then drove back to the lodge and prepared for supper, which was highlighted by meat taken from the game a few of the hunters had killed during the day. We ended the evening by sharing stories and drinking wine. There was lots of laughter.

A weather front came through during the night, so Monday morning was very cold. I wore gloves and a hat pulled down over my ears. Rob's son, Luca, went with us and wore short pants, and so did Rob. They both nearly froze during the day. We ended up sitting on a wooded hilltop for an hour, and later sat out in the open on the side of a hill in a strong wind that made it seem even colder. The kudus and oryx we were hunting spent the whole morning standing behind large bushes and under thick-leaved trees to stay out of the wind. They were very hard to see because they didn't move much. We had stalked a few of those animals over the last two days, and they always seemed to disappear in the vegetation just as we got within rifle range.

During the morning, Jim took aim at a large male kudu across a valley on a far hillside 325 yards away. The wind was blowing so hard that his rifle, which was braced on the bamboo tripod, could not be held steady. He missed with two separate shots before the kudu vanished in the thick underbrush.

We then moved back to the truck and drove up a very rough, rock strewn and washed out road until three light gray oryx were seen on a distant hillside surrounded by green vegetation. We quietly walked toward the area until we were some 500 yards away. At that time, the three oryx began to get nervous. They moved out of the open area. Soon they disappeared. Jim really wanted to shoot one of those animals because the long straight horns and the fur colors were so fantastic. The wind was still blowing very hard, and we had been told that Cape Town, on the southwestern tip of South Africa, had received snow over the night. That indicated how cold it was.

After lunch, we went back out at 3:00. It was still cold and extremely windy. While standing on the top of a ridge and observing kudus in the distance, the wind was blowing so hard I kept losing my hat. I found it hard to stand up straight and focus my eyes through the binoculars.

We saw kudus, oryx, red hartebeests, blue wildebeests, zebras, blesboks, black wildebeests, impalas and many others during the day's outing. They stayed a great distance from us or quickly hid in the underbrush surrounded by thick trees on the hillsides as we approached.

At 5:00 we realized there was only about one hour of hunting time left. We decided to travel to a flat area on a mountain top and try to separate a big male blesbok from the herd. We approached the area, and a group of 250 to 300 of them began to run away when they saw our vehicle a quarter mile away. Rob decided that Tami should take the four-wheel drive and circle around behind the herd and trick them into running by us, as we hid behind a large clump of trees growing alone in the middle of the huge span of open land. That didn't work, so we tried to approach them on foot. Every time we were within 400 yards, the herd would stampede and circle in an area far away. That became very frustrating, mainly because it was getting dark, and the cold wind was still blowing hard. We were beginning to realize that tracking and shooting that species would not be as easy as the first two days had been with the other game.

Tuesday morning the wind finally let up, but it was still cold. After breakfast, we drove to the same hillside area we had hunted the last two days. Jim was determined to get a big kudu. For two hours the skies spit light rain, and a dark, low hanging cloud carrying a gray mist filled the valley. At one point it became so foggy that we could hardly see the large mountain ranges in the distance. Rob spotted a dark, chocolate-brown male bushbuck at the bottom of the valley approximately 300 yards away, but determined its horns were not long enough for a nice trophy mount. We later glassed the opposite hillside from 400 to 500 yards and saw many female kudus. We were only interested in the males with long horns, so we moved to another spot.

We traveled down the hill about a third of the way, and the sun popped through the clouds long enough to bring a couple of young male kudus out to tempt us. Rob would not let Jim take a shot at either of them. He wanted one with much longer horns, where the pointed tips curled on the final twist toward the front. That was a definite sign of a mature male, and we wanted to find one.

As we looked across to a faraway hillside, we spotted a small oryx, a warthog and a huge male waterbuck. The waterbuck sported a large rack of backward curved horns and was obviously an old male. He never got closer than 400 yards, which was too far to attempt a shot. Off in the distance, more than a half a mile away, we could see five zebras and three large oryx. We decided to try and focus on shooting one of the male oryx the next day. Their horns formed a large "V" as they angled upwards off the crown of the head.

It would soon be lunchtime, so we left that area and climbed through the underbrush on our way back to the truck. It was a tiring climb. We had to dodge lots of small cacti and large thorn bushes. Those bushes and tree limbs forced us to get extra exercise while we ducked and weaved our way up the rise.

While we drove along the dusty, clay colored road with short grass and large stones in the center, Rob suddenly stopped the car and grabbed his binoculars. On a hillside, near an area of thick cover, was a large male kudu standing in a very small clearing. It was what we had been trying to find. He was standing and showing off his large rack of horns and beautiful face with the white band running over the bridge of his nose. Jim jumped from the vehicle while Rob quickly set up the bamboo tripod, so Jim could get a shot before the kudu disappeared into the underbrush. I checked my range finder, and the distance was 234 yards. As Jim sighted his rifle's scope and readied for the shot, I watched intently through my binoculars. His gun went off. The kudu jumped and headed down the hillside. It was instantly lost in the bush. We didn't know if it had been hit, but Jim, Rob, Tami and I started walking in that direction to start tracking the animal. Jim felt he had hit the kudu, but sometimes after being hit, they would run a long way and get lost in the brush before falling.

Rob asked Jim and me to circle around and walk toward a dirt road on the top of the rise, so if the kudu had crossed we could possibly spot blood drops on the ground. Rob and Tami walked directly through the thick brush and saw blood. They knew for sure it had been hit. Within ten minutes, Rob yelled and told us they had found it. Upon observation, it was a mature male with a large set of trophy horns. Tami was then told to drive our truck to the lodge and pick up three men to come and help get the large animal loaded into the vehicle. Before leaving the spot for the afternoon, Jim and I went to take a final look. I took a series of photos under a cloud covered sky. After three days of hard hunting, he had finally killed a fantastic male kudu. We knew it would make a wonderful mount for his home. The shot had been taken at 12:30. By the time we arrived back at the lodge for lunch, it was after 3:00. We were all tired and called it a "good day of hunting." Afterwards, we stayed at the lodge to rest.

The next morning, after an early breakfast, we bundled up and started out. It was still cold and windy. The clouds hung tightly to the mountain tops in the distance, and there was the same gray fog in the valley as the day before. As we drove to our first hunting site for the day, we spotted three oryx in the sunlight on a hillside. Because of the heavy brush and trees, our only shot would be if they wandered down lower on the hill within 200 to 300 yards. We watched them through our binoculars for at least an hour and a half. They only moved 150 yards to the left. We knew if we tried to climb the hill where we would be level with them, they would probably disappear into the thickets.

Rob suggested we give up on them and move some distance away to see if we could single out a big male from a roaming herd of blesboks. We had tried that once before and had failed. The animals had huge expanses of land on which to run, and when in a herd there were many eyes watching our approach.

It seemed our only hope of getting a male blesbok was to position ourselves in the middle of a huge open savannah near an isolated clump of green bushes. Tami took the vehicle and drove around to the backside of the herd. As Tami drove off through the brown grass and around an endless number of termite mounds, I lay down on the ground and fell asleep. Jim and Rob remained alert, and they waited to see if any blesboks would be tricked by the truck and run in our direction.

It took almost two hours, but the blesboks finally showed up. Rob and Jim woke me, and I slid around to the backside of the bushes while staying low. The herd ran hard toward us until they were 200 yards away, and then the leaders just stopped. As they all hesitated, Rob helped Jim pick out a nice old male with large horns. Once that one was selected, Jim took aim off the makeshift tripod, and a loud gunshot followed. The big male hit the ground immediately. The rest of them ran at least a half mile before stopping.

Jim asked me to use the sighting device, which measured accurately the distance in yards using a laser beam. The distance that came up for his shot was 194 yards. As we approached the fallen animal, we could tell the shot had hit it perfectly in the shoulder for a quick kill. The animal was rolled over and set up so we could take some photos. We then got it loaded and drove back to the lodge for lunch.

Lunch was spaghetti with chopped hamburger meat. We added some sweet chili sauce that made it really good. We rested for an hour while we talked about the morning's experiences and were then out again by 4:00 for another hunt. We didn't have any luck the first hour. At 5:00 we received a cell phone call from one of the other hunters. He had wounded a large oryx and needed our help to track it through the thick underbrush using Casey's ability to pick up the scent.

We arrived at the area with less than an hour of daylight left. We had two Jack Russell terriers with us, Casey and Miller. As we stepped down from the truck, we could see the other three hunters in the distance and talked to them by using a walkie-talkie. They told us they could see the wounded oryx running sporadically through the trees and underbrush, but couldn't get close enough to take a final shot. Rob and Tami moved to cut it off before it crossed the dirt road running up the hill. Rob told Jim and me to stay where we were, so as to not get in the line of fire.

It wasn't long before we heard gun shots, a total of six, and then the two small dogs started barking. We knew that was a sure sign the animal was on the ground. Rob yelled to us from 200 yards and told us to come over to see the oryx. As Jim and I approached, I could hardly believe the beauty and interesting color patterns and markings on the animal. We saw it was a large female. In that species, both the male and female have long straight horns, but the male's horns are slightly thicker and closer together at the base of the head. Her long straight horns were measured at 34 inches.

After I took many photos, the men loaded the animal into the back of Rob's truck. As we drove away, I realized it was completely dark, and we needed headlights to see the rough road. We arrived back at the lodge at 7:00. The skinners were ready to start stripping the hide of the oryx for later mounting. Four men worked together to accomplish that, while their wives finished the preparation of our food for dinner. Keith told us the workers lived in a separate building near the lodge and had been with him as a coordinated team for many years.

Thursday morning started off quickly. It was a little warmer, so we didn't have to wear as many clothes as the previous two days and definitely no gloves. A mile from the lodge, Rob spotted a nice male mountain reedbok alongside two evenly colored females standing on a cliffside in the shade. When the three of them moved into the sunlight, it became obvious how beautiful their coloring was. They were about the size of a German Shepherd but with horns.

Rob, Tami and Jim moved within 165 yards to set up for the shot. I stayed back on the other ridge. From that distance, I would not scare the reedbok. Jim's shot was clean and the animal went down. After the shot, the two females quickly ran off, up and over a ridge, and disappeared. We took photos and carried the animal back to the parked truck. Jim decided he would have a full body mount done by the taxidermist. Rob told us we should drive back to the lodge, so the waiting animal skinners could get started on the delicate skin before it cooled.

With everything loaded, we drove to the lodge where we spent a couple of hours eating lunch and sharing stories around the large dining room table.

After lunch, we had an eventful afternoon hunting for oryx. Keith had arranged for us to travel fifteen miles to another land owner's property who thought he had a few oryx up in the hills. We arrived at his place around 4:00 and began to drive down a long dirt road toward the mountains in the distance. After searching for some time, we located five oryx in a group. For thirty minutes, they kept a distance of 400 yards between us. We finally narrowed that distance to 320 yards, and Jim set up for a shot. He had been shooting high on the previous two animals. It turned out that when he had adjusted his scope, he hadn't realized that two clicks on the scope magnified at 300 yards. He decided in order to bring his shot to a lower position, he needed to give the scope six clicks. That turned out to be way too much adjustment. When he took his first shot, it hit the oryx too low in the bottom of the stomach. The animal did not go down. We knew it had been hit, but the oryx was so large and heavy it was hard to bring down unless the shot was perfect.

The five oryx ran together over a hilltop into the distance, while Casey and Miller were sent to pick up the blood trail. We hurried down a long hillside and weaved around thorn bushes that were as tall as a man and dodged low lying cactus plants that were everywhere. Their needles would stick to your shoe soles and pants and then stick into your legs. That was very painful and happened to me many times. As we tracked the wounded oryx, both Casey and Miller constantly yipped because of the small bundles of needles that stuck in their skin.

Miller, the younger terrier, was soon balled up on the ground with so many cactus balls stuck to his body he could hardly move. I turned and went back to him, as everyone else continued in the direction of the oryx, to see if I could help him. He had cactus needles stuck to the front of his head between his eyes. He also had them stuck in his tongue, the roof of his mouth and his gums. All four feet and legs were full of the sharp points. I pulled out as many as I could find from his body and in ten minutes had him ready to go. I felt sorry for him, because there were so many cacti on the property where we were hunting. I picked him up and carried him for the next mile. By that time, I was so far behind the others, I had no idea where they had gone while tracking the wounded oryx.

I soon heard, through the woods and down in the valley, two gun shots in quick succession. That gave me an idea of which way to go, but the echo through the valley could have easily led me in the wrong direction. As I walked, I searched the area and soon saw everyone together across a valley on a distant hillside. Jim called for me and told me to catch up. As I crossed a washed out ravine in the valley, while carrying Miller, I heard an additional two shots fired farther up the ridge. By the time I arrived at the scene, the oryx was dead on the ground. I marveled at the beauty of the animal. The patterns and markings were definitely

striking on the body, and its face was full of strong white, chocolate, tan and brown areas with some almost black. The side of
the body was a soft gray. The horns were long and straight and
measured 35 inches from the top of the head. In my opinion,
the oryx is so unusual and beautiful it should be the symbol for
Africa, but most everyone relates to lions, elephants and impalas
when they think of Africa.

Just before sunset, we loaded the oryx in the truck after a
series of photos were taken. The sunset was so colorful that
we stopped the truck and took photos of the sky until the sun
was completely gone below the horizon. We arrived back at the
lodge an hour later and left the oryx with the skinners. They
were instructed to prepare the skin, head and horns so the taxidermist could later make a head and shoulder mount. Jim and
I talked about how impressive that mount would be, with the
exceptional colors and very long, black horns.

We had set up the lynx hunt for the next morning. It would
take place, using dogs, on another property an hour's drive away.
We would be getting up before 5:00 and leaving the lodge around
6:00. It promised to be another exciting hunt. We understood
there were many lynx on the sheep farmer's land. The farmers in
the area all wanted to get rid of them. The lynx constantly killed
their sheep, and as a result, they welcomed hunters who wanted
to harvest them for mounts.

Upon waking, I realized it was Friday the 13th. I was unsure
if it would be a lucky day or not. The plan was to meet the land-
owner at 7:00 where he would have his dogs. As we arrived, the
owner and his son drove up with eight hunting dogs loaded in
the back of an old pickup truck. The dogs were barking loudly
and ready to go. We got out of our truck and surveyed the area
that had different typography from where we had been hunting.
The mountains were much steeper, the valleys much deeper and
everything was very green in all directions. The man explained
he owned 4,000 acres and farmed sheep for a living. As I looked

around, I could see many groups of adults and babies scattered over the hills, appearing as white specks in the distance.

The owner's son unloaded the eight red and white hunting dogs and starting walking with them down the ridge, following a fence that ran down into the valley. The owner walked with Rob, Jim and me as we went around the hilltop in another direction to the left. Father and son were talking back and forth using walkie-talkies. The dogs yipped and barked occasionally as they worked through the thick brush. Gradually their barking became harder to hear, as they went farther into the deep valley below.

The lynx hunt reminded me of a coon hunt in Tennessee. The dogs did most of the work by picking up a scent and following it until the animal was eventually treed. Once up in the tree, the hunters would come along and shoot it.

While we were descending one side of the mountain, the owner's son called us from the opposite side and told us to go toward the noise of the barking dogs. We could hear them in the distance, and we were told they probably had a lynx in a tree. We finally worked our way down the steep hillside while stumbling over loose stones. We reached the dried up creek bed and started up the other side with anticipation. The tallest tree held a cinnamon colored lynx with black tuffs pointing upwards off each ear. I had heard that if the hunters made too much noise, the lynx would jump out of the tree and escape. We didn't want that to happen, so we all remained quiet with the only noise being that of the dogs barking as they ran around the base of the tree.

Jim loaded a shotgun and took one clean shot from 60 feet with buck shot. The lynx immediately fell from the tree and died before we could get over and take a look. It was a female weighing approximately 25 pounds and the size of a medium dog. There were distinctive markings on its face that included cream and black patches running from the nose to its ears. Its teeth were white and the claws were very sharp. I realized what I had been told earlier was true, that those predators could easily kill a small sheep each day. Rob told us the lynx never saved a carcass and had to kill for fresh meat daily. The sheepherders wanted to get rid of as many of them as possible. They were glad to see us interested in hunting them.

The lynx was carried down to a dirt road at the base of the hill, where we took a series of photos as we had done with all the other animals. We then drove out of the valley after everything was loaded into the truck. I was glad, because I was not looking forward to climbing back up the steep hill we had earlier come down.

In the afternoon, we drove to a river that flowed through the property a few miles from the lodge. It was lined by thick trees and low bushes. Our goal was to locate a nice old bushbuck. That was the kind of habitat where they could be found. After an unsuccessful two hours of glassing, we left and went to a mountain top that overlooked a long valley and glassed the opposite hillside 250 yards away. We located two males and one female bushbuck on a far mountainside. We determined that unless one of the males started moving up the steep slope, we wouldn't be able to get him out before dark if we did kill him. We decided to come back in the morning when the sun was up. At that time, we would see if we could locate one of the male bushbucks a little higher on the ridge.

On Saturday morning, there was no wind and the birds were chirping. It promised to be a warm day to find a nice bushbuck. On our way to the mountain ridge, we searched for another horned animal called a steenbok. Those were small deerlike animals with small black horns six to seven inches long. The steenboks were fast, and once startled, they ran away very quickly. Their color was a rusty-cinnamon brown. We saw a couple of females, but no males, and the male was the only one we were after.

We reached our spot for the morning bushbuck hunt and started down a steep ridge just as the sun began to hit the far side of the mountain. We walked as far down the hill as we could safely navigate and began to glass the area. I looked down below my feet and realized that all four of us were standing on the very edge of a rock bluff that dropped off dramatically to a valley floor far below.

After 30 minutes, Rob spotted two male bushbucks on the ridge across the valley. Tami watched with him, and I checked the distance with the hand-held laser scope, which checked out to be 284 yards. The sun began to light up more of the hillside as the two bushbucks began to graze on the leaves of a small tree in full sunlight. We were still positioned in the shade as the bushbucks worked their way slowly in and out of the thick brush and small open areas. The wind was light and the air was getting warmer by the moment. We continued to glass the valley for other options, but kept coming back to those two fully mature bushbucks. In the sunlight, we could see clearly the dark brown chocolate fur and the nice horns on each of them. They had white coloring on their legs and white dots on their flanks. Overall, they were quite impressive.

The decision was made to take a shot, from a little under 300 yards, at the larger of the two bushbucks. Jim positioned the bamboo tripod on the cliff edge and lowered his rifle onto its top in preparation. I watched silently from a sitting position on a large rock and wondered how accurately Jim could shoot from that distance. The seconds ticked away slowly. I held my breath as I waited for the shot.

When the gun fired, the animal reacted by jumping upward. It then tumbled down the hill 20 feet. Immediately, it leaped to its right 30 feet and disappeared behind thick underbrush and trees. We kept our binoculars sighted on the area to see if the animal ran under the tall bushes trying to escape. There was no other movement, except for the second bushbuck hurrying its way along the ridge putting distance between us and it.

We waited ten minutes, and finally Rob sent Tami around the

mountaintop to check and see if the animal was indeed down permanently. Jim, Rob and I remained in our location. That way we were able to direct Tami by yelling and using hand signals pointing to the location where we had last seen the bushbuck. Tami soon reached the area and signaled back that we should come over. We slowly walked back up the mountainside until we reached the truck. We drove over very rough terrain until we got as close as we could to the other hilltop. From there, we walked down the hill. The bushbuck was lying on its side when we arrived, and Tami was smiling. The shot had hit perfectly through the shoulder for a quick kill. From close to 300 yards, I thought it was pretty unusual. Jim had a big smile on his face when I looked over at him.

The next chore was to get the animal up the hillside and loaded in the truck. I estimated it weighed between 150 to 165 pounds. Rob surprised me by saying he would load it on his shoulders and carry it out himself. I didn't think that was possible because of the weight of the animal and the steep incline, but Rob loaded it onto his shoulders and started up the long steep hillside all on his own. He only stopped once to catch his breath and rest briefly. When we got to the top, Tami and Rob positioned the bushbuck so we could take photos. The bushbuck was another beautiful animal, and probably the last one on Jim's list for our hunting trip.

We arrived back at the lodge by 10:30. The skinners immediately got to work. Jim asked the men to skin out the animal, so it could be a full mount.

We left the lodge at 3:45 that afternoon for one last drive over the nearby landscape. There were groups of monkeys, baboons, unusual rodents that looked like small kangaroos called spring hares, porcupines, rabbits, tortoises and other creatures that we had wanted to see again. One of the small animals we still hoped to locate was a gray duiker. It was our last evening of hunting, so we decided to give it a try before the sun went down. After an hour of searching, we saw a mature male all by itself near a washed out ravine. It stopped after a short run and stood broadside 215 yards from us. Jim set up the tripod for his last shot, while I stayed in the vehicle with Stiffie, another one of Rob's sons, who came with us on the final day. I didn't want to spook the animal by mistake. Jim's shot was perfect, and the gray duiker was retrieved and brought to the truck.

As we drove back toward the lodge after our final evening of hunting, the sunset was tremendous. The low hanging clouds near the horizon turned a bright crimson color when the sun was totally down. Above, the sky was a dark blue and all those colors met the completely black silhouetted tree line. What a nice scene it was to end the day and our hunting safari!

Sunday morning we drove two hours southwest to the Addo Elephant National Park. I was told there were 400 to 500 elephants and many Cape buffalos located within the park, along with many other unusual African animals we had not seen.

As we drove along the main highway and began to get close to the elephant park, we saw high fences that were hooked up electrically. Then we began to see a few herds of different African animals. There were pastures, hillsides and brush forests. The rainfall must have been heavier there, since everything was much greener.

We pulled into the park and Rob went in to buy our tickets. He told the ticket person we were all from South Africa, so the cost for everyone was only $30. If he had admitted two of us were Americans, the cost would have been $90. We started driving through the open park in our own vehicle, and soon spotted our first adult elephant standing just beside the dusty road eating a small bush with the help of his trunk. We took some nice close-up photos before the elephant disappeared through the thick vegetation. We meandered along the road that worked its way through the park on our self-guided tour. Rob knew many facts about the area and its animals. He shared interesting bits of information as we moved along.

We saw a few cars in the distance that had stopped at a waterhole and wondered what everyone was looking at. As we got closer, we realized there were two males and one female lion lying on the ground just in front of one of the stopped cars. Everyone was taking close-up photos while sitting in their cars. We had been told not to exit our cars on the drive through. After getting close and taking some good digital pictures, we moved along and quickly discovered red hartebeests, blesboks and other animals in small groups close to the road. We had been told the park contained 200 square miles of open land for the animals to roam.

Because of the dense vegetation and open space, it was a wonder we saw as many animals as we did. There were large mature horned kudus, elands, springboks, jackals, yellow mongooses, land tortoises, meerkats, Cape buffalos, zebras, giraffes, impalas and elephants scattered everywhere in singles and in herds. The large bull elephants were most impressive in their natural environment. In the distance, we noticed one of them having a scuffle with a younger male, pushing him away from the females. They were being very aggressive toward each other with lots of ear flapping and kicking of dust with their feet and trunks. Eventually, after a short standoff, the older elephant seemed to win the contest. The smaller male then went off on his own.

We passed a curve in the road and spotted a few meerkats running around. I mentioned to Rob the series on the Animal Planet channel from a few years earlier about a meerkat family ruled by a female named Daisy. Rob told us the series had been filmed there at the Addo Elephant National Park, and we were probably viewing some of Daisy's family running around.

We left the park in time to get back to Woodlands for our last night at the lodge. The trip to the park had been a great experience and a nice way to end our African adventure.

*"It is good to have an end
to journey toward, but it is the journey
that matters in the end."*

Ernest Hemingway

China
April 2011

My younger brother, Jim, called me one day in the fall of 2010 and asked if I would be interested in making a trip to China. At the time, I had never considered I might be able to travel to such a different and exotic place. After thinking about it for only a short time, I decided I would go. The decision was made easily because I didn't think I would ever have another chance to see that country.

Jim told me, "I need to go to the Canton Business Fair, west of the city of Hong Kong. I want to check on possibly importing some items in bulk that are produced very cheaply in factories across China, and retail them to my customers. I already have a good friend who does that regularly. He has all of the connections worked out."

I said, "That sounds good to me. Let's go check it out together. I would love to see that country and its people. I'd also like to experience the culture."

I found out that J.R., Jim's friend, would normally make two to three business trips to China each year. He knew exactly what to do in order to get his purchased products transported back to the United States in large containers, which would be carried by ships across the ocean. Jim told me he could do the same thing, with the help of J.R., and he thought he could make a nice profit on what he shipped back.

It sounded interesting to me, so we made the travel arrangements. I was personally assisted in working out many of the details with Trent's help, who had always been very good at setting up my travels. We scheduled the trip for the middle of April in 2011.

My first plane ride took me from Wilmington to Nashville, where I met up with Jim and J.R. From there, we flew to New York for a layover and a plane change. We boarded the flight to Beijing and were excited about our upcoming adventure to that foreign land. I knew the plane ride to China was going to take more time in the air than Jim and I had endured when we traveled to South Africa in 2010. As it turned out, including all of the layovers at the airports and the three different plane flights, it took me a total of thirty-three hours to get there, with the last flight taking eighteen hours by itself.

We were going into a country where we could not speak the language and would need an interpreter. J.R. had assured us he would take care of all the details by hooking us up with all of his previously established business connections. That included an interpreter who would be provided by a company he normally worked with.

He told us he had developed a strong relationship with a large manufacturer in China that served as a middle man for him. A division of that company specialized in getting purchased items shipped back to America for businessmen like J.R. The people he worked with helped us with hotel reservations, car rentals and recommended various restaurants. There was no question J.R.'s help and connections were needed, and over the next two weeks they were invaluable as we moved around the country.

When we first landed in Beijing, we were all exhausted. After checking into a very fancy hotel in the downtown area, we quickly went to our rooms and slept for twelve hours. Because of the time change, we knew it would be days before our biological clocks got back on track. Our days and nights were certainly out of sync. With the passage of time, we knew that would all straighten out.

The next day, we ate in the hotel in Beijing where we were staying. It had a five star restaurant on the top floor serving many items of which I was familiar. Chicken was a popular dish and was served in many different ways, along with many assorted vegetables and fruits such as watermelon, cantaloupe and honeydew. There were fish dishes, breads and plenty of interesting tasty sauces. Overall, they had a little of everything we could have wanted in an elegant restaurant that catered to foreign tourists.

Jim and I stayed in the city that day and walked around the streets just to observe the people. J.R. met with a few of the companies with which he had relationships.

Beijing was a city of twenty-seven million people, and there were many large buildings lining the major roads in every direction. The area in which we were staying looked like New York City, but larger. There was much to see. We mainly just used that first day to adjust from our long and exhausting trip.

I had asked J.R. how many people lived in the entire country of China. He told me he thought there were around one and a quarter billion people. As I thought about that, I realized what a huge number it was. The United States had just over three hundred and ten million. China had about four times as many people as we did on a similar size land mass.

On the second day, we went back to the airport and flew approximately three hours to Hong Kong, which was located to the south but still on the east coast of China. Hong Kong was another very large city with a population of around twenty-three million. It looked something like Beijing with all of the large buildings but was more spread out and didn't seem to be as modern.

We were to have our first big meal in Hong Kong the following evening. J.R. had contacted the owner of the main company he worked with in that city, and we were invited out to dinner. Jim wasn't feeling well. He decided not to go with us and just get something simple at the in-house restaurant. I was hungry, so I decided to go to dinner with J.R. and his business friend.

The friend was a nice man who picked us up at the hotel in

his Mercedes. After introductions, we traveled a few miles to a Chinese restaurant that was one of his favorites. On the way, we passed many retail stores with colorful neon lights and large glass fronts with signs I could not read. People were everywhere. The sidewalks bordering the main road were covered with them. Most of them were walking, but a few people were riding bicycles at the edge of the road. The major roadway was full of traffic and contained up to six lanes going in each direction.

I quickly noticed how much smog was in the air. It was dense and looked like gray smoke. I didn't think much about it at first, but later realized it never went away. There were a few people walking on the sidewalk who wore face masks, and I thought that was strange. Later I realized they were individuals who were concerned about their health and didn't want to constantly breathe the highly polluted air.

When we arrived at the restaurant, I noticed there were cages, plastic tubs and tables set up out front with all kinds of displayed items. We were expected to pick out what we wanted to eat before entering the restaurant from an array of live critters and garden products. It was like walking through a farmer's market. As we passed that area, our host told us, in easy to understand English, to pick out what we wanted to eat for our meal. I was surprised, because I had never experienced that type of restaurant and became interested in looking at what was offered.

On the tables were all kinds of vegetables. The selection included tomatoes, cucumbers, onions, corn, radishes, beans, potatoes, and lettuce. Sitting on the pavement in front of the tables were deep, plastic tubs containing live frogs, turtles, eels, different species of fish, lobsters, crabs and other interesting creatures. All of those were crowded together and crawling all over each other inside their containers.

To the left side were cages holding live chickens. The most disgusting thing I saw that night were cages containing small dogs and cats. Each of those animals looked like one of my past pets and stared up at me with sad eyes. Apparently they were being offered to customers to be eaten for supper. That shocked me and almost made me sick.

I asked the man who had taken us to the restaurant, "Do they really serve those friendly and intelligent animals as food?"

He replied, "I never eat them myself, but some people do, especially in this province of Guangzhou located west of Hong Kong. Throughout most of China, it is not as popular as it is here."

Once I heard that comment, I wasn't as hungry. My selection included a fish, which was instantly removed from the tub where it was swimming, along with some assorted vegetables and fruit. Our host picked some vegetables and a chicken that was quickly removed from its cage. Before we had taken many steps toward the front door, the chicken's neck was twisted off and blood drained freely to the pavement. I was sick to my stomach before we even entered the building.

Within thirty minutes, we were served our items on a Lazy Susan table where the platters rotated around in front of us. We were invited to sample other items which we hadn't picked out. My choice of a fish was served on a platter with its head still attached and eyes wide open. It was sitting up on its opened belly with the scales still on the skin. After the original shock of the presentation, I settled down and ate small amounts of most everything. Overall, the food was good. I had some tea along with my meal.

To our enjoyment, some live music was played after the dinner. As we left the restaurant, the owner came over to bow and thanked each of us for coming. All I could think about, during and after the meal, were those dogs and cats in the cages outside. I wondered if any of them had been chosen that evening by a customer.

When I arrived back at the room, the first thing I told Jim was, "You should be glad that you didn't go to eat with us. If you had gone, you would be feeling even worse than you are now."

I proceeded to tell him about the strange way the items had been presented out in front of the restaurant.

After telling him about the tubs full of all kinds of creatures and what was in the larger cages, he said, "You've got to be kidding. They were offering dogs and cats for food?"

I answered, "Yes, it was terrible. I almost couldn't eat my fish."

The next day we drove by car to the Canton Business Fair. It was located in huge, eight-story buildings west of Hong Kong. The buildings were multiple structures that each extended for what looked like a quarter of a mile. They were lined up in rows specifically constructed for the fair that occurred twice each year, in the spring and in the fall.

The fair showcased all of the major factories and their products which were produced across the country, so buyers from around the world could come and purchase a large variety from one location at very cheap wholesale prices. We were told there were as many as 75,000 trade show booths spread throughout the buildings representing all the factories. We soon found out it involved many hours to check out each one of them.

Our assigned interpreter for the day joined us for the ride to the fair. She was twenty-four years old and could speak four languages. She spoke English very well and told us that for the past twenty-two years her country had required English to be taught in their schools starting at kindergarten and going all the way through graduation. As a result, all of the younger people we ran into could communicate with us to some degree. Those who were over twenty-five years old were able to speak to us only in broken sentences, and communication was difficult or impossible.

We entered the fair with our name tags around our necks and joined the large crowds mingling with the booth vendors. Our interpreter pulled a two wheeled metal cart so she could carry anything we wanted to take with us. As the day wore on, that included hundreds of heavy, glossy paper brochures telling about the items we looked at in each booth and how to go about ordering them.

We walked from booth to booth and quickly passed those we were not interested in checking out. Whenever we saw something of interest, we would ask a few questions while communicating through the interpreter, then look at samples and afterwards obtain a business card and brochure. The booths were lined up side by side with as many as ten rows on each floor.

Even though the main buildings were extremely long, the individual areas on each floor were partitioned off about every hundred yards by internal walls that forced all the visitors to go from floor to floor to see everything. Every new area we entered contained different products. When we were interested in seeing a particular type of item, we would follow the signs and go directly to that location.

We learned the spring Canton Business Fair was to continue for fifteen days. After our first full day of walking and visiting hundreds of booths, we realized it might take that much time to see it all. We left with a cart full of brochures and some general knowledge of what to expect the following day.

Early the next morning, we repeated what we had done the day before. We slowly worked our way through the enormous buildings and covered all eight floors in each area. It was all interesting to see, and the variety of products seemed endless. Of particular interest were the LED lighting areas. That type of lighting had been popular for only a few years, and China seemed to lead the world in a diversity of ways to use it. We saw special low voltage LED lights for warehouses, for advertising signs, for homes, for Christmas decorations and for many other uses.

From that area, we next entered a section for toys. We moved from booth to booth and observed the many different products that were offered to world buyers to be purchased in bulk. The vendors would not sell just a few of a particular product. We found they might give us a single sample, if they thought we were really interested. To purchase anything, we were expected to order a minimum of a few thousand up to ten thousand units, depending on the overall cost. Everything had to be loaded in large containers to be carried on ships traveling across the ocean to get to the United States. It would be weeks or months before those containers would arrive. That delay of time had to be taken into consideration, especially in regard to seasonal products, such as those used at Christmas.

Each day, when we arrived back at our room, we discussed how far we had walked at the fair. We figured we had walked approximately five miles each day. After the first seven days, we were sure we had traveled at least thirty-five miles while looking at the individual booths and their products. We had amassed a huge pile of brochures and multiple samples for later consideration. As we talked about it, the conclusion was that we had probably seen only one-third of the entire show in the past seven days.

J.R., Jim and I decided that even though the fair would continue for the entire next week, we were exhausted and ready to do something different. A few of the vendors had invited us to travel to their factories for plant tours, so we decided to take advantage of a couple of those opportunities to see how the products were made. Since I created sculptures and worked with bronze foundries in the United States, I wanted to take a tour to one of the companies that made bronze sculptures in bulk. I was interested to see how inexpensively I could get items made in China and shipped back home.

The first factory visit was set up, and the next day a car pulled up with a driver and a young female interpreter inside. Jim had asked for the largest car they could provide, being a large man with a bad back. The car that was waiting was a luxury vehicle, but not very big. After voicing a complaint, Jim got in the front and pushed the passenger seat completely back against the back seat. His knees were still against the dash board. He was obviously uncomfortable and unhappy.

After twenty miles on the busy 12 lane interstate road, Jim told the driver he had to stop so he could get out and stretch. Because the guy didn't speak English, he continued on down the road until Jim let us know that his cramped position was cutting off the circulation in his legs. When we finally got the driver to pull off the road, Jim was in trouble and barely able to get out of the car. I felt sorry for him. The interpreter told us the car was the largest one available in that area. The Chinese were much smaller than us. That difference was reflected in the size of their automobiles.

As we continued on our way, I began a conversation with the interpreter who was very willing to talk.

I asked her, "How often do you travel away from your home in Hong Kong?"

She told me, "I've never been as far away as we are now from the city."

At that time we were only about thirty miles west.

I then asked her, "What about the air pollution?   The air seems to always be hazy with thick smog everywhere."

She responded, "One of these days I want to travel to the United States, because in my lifetime I have never seen a clear blue sky or the sun, except through a haze. I've only seen those things in photos from places like your country. I'm always looking through this dense pollution when I look upward.   The factories here all burn coal for energy, and the resulting smog that fills the air is terrible.   It even affects the rivers and the water supply everywhere in China.   It is all extremely polluted."

I was surprised at those comments.   I had already thought about how bad it must be to continually breathe the air.   I knew I would only be there for two weeks so maybe it would not present a problem for me, as far as my health.   For the people who lived there all the time, there was no doubt that after a few years it would be a health concern.

I asked her about the crowded roads and she replied, "It wasn't long ago that many of the people here in the city either walked or rode bicycles. Only in the last twenty years have small cars become available at a price the working middle class could afford."

I said to her, "The roads are all extremely wide with heavy traffic, and all the lanes are completely full."

She told me, "If your family owns a car, you can only drive it one day a week. The first number on your license plate determines which day you are allowed on the road. For instance, if the number one appears first on your plate, then you can be on the road with your car on Monday. If the number two appears first on your plate, then you can be on the road only on Tuesday, etc. You have to get all your shopping and driving done on the day you are assigned, or otherwise you must walk or ride a bicycle."

That conversation left me speechless.

After a moment, I asked her about the large clusters of tall buildings positioned around the city. Each building I referred to was fifty to sixty stories high with ten to twelve of them in a cluster. All were circular in design, with units around the outer sides, and had glassed openings with small balconies.

She explained, "Those are where the middle class workers live. They contain many small units of about one thousand square feet and are usually owned by a husband and wife with one child, plus a grandmother and grandfather. The grandparents usually take care of the one child, which is all the government allows, and the younger couple works outside the home to provide the income."

I asked her, "How much does one of those small units cost?"

She said, "Each unit is priced at around three hundred and fifty thousand dollars and with all the people living in it, everything is cramped. They are just glad to be able to make the payments."

Then I asked her, "Tell me more about the government and families only being able to have one child."

She replied, "Sometime in the past, they decided that China's population was too large. A law was passed that every new family was allowed to have only one child. After having that one child, if the wife became pregnant again, she would be immediately transported to a hospital for an abortion. That decision was completely taken out of the family's control. We have all come to accept that handling by the government."

She followed up by saying, "There is a preference for a male child in this country. Sometimes when it is discovered by ultra sound that the mother is carrying a female, she may choose to have an abortion. The government allows that decision. The thinking is that males are more productive individuals throughout their lifetimes."

I found all of that information very disturbing.

It was lunch time, and we decided to stop for something to eat. Jim and I had eaten throughout the week at various restaurants where we had to choose what we wanted to eat outside before entering. That seemed to be standard for the high end restaurants around the city. On that day, we were looking for something different. The only American places we saw were franchises for McDonalds or Kentucky Fried Chicken. We picked a McDonalds and entered the doors ready to enjoy something familiar.

The restaurant offered only a condensed version of the foods we normally get in America. There were pictures of a Big Mac, double cheese burger, fish sandwich and French fries, with sodas from a machine. Each of us chose a Big Mac with fries and a Diet Coke and sat down to enjoy our meal.

I asked the young girl with us if she regularly came to McDonalds to eat and she replied, "Never."

I said, "Why don't you come to this restaurant? It's so quick and cheap?"

She replied, "This is very expensive food and considered a luxury. What you just paid for my meal of about eight dollars is almost what I make in an entire week working as an interpreter."

I was shocked to hear what she had just said, but understood. It was obvious she was living in extreme poverty. Later, when we dropped her off at her home in the evening, that fact became even clearer. She had a big smile on her face as she slowly consumed the burger, fries and drink. Afterwards, she thanked us for buying her food.

When we arrived at the bronze factory, we were told to sit in the lobby to wait for the owner who would show us around. Finally he appeared and a tray of tea was put in front of us. The owner served each of us using small china cups. We had a short conversation before we were allowed to go through his facility. That was apparently the tradition and the way they greeted their visitors. Until we made small talk and drank tea, we would not be allowed to see his factory.

Afterwards, we went through his business and saw examples of what his workers normally made. Lots of the items were reproductions of pieces originally made in America or other countries, and they were reproducing them in bulk without paying the artist for the rights. I asked about the cost of individual items. I learned it was ten times lower than it would cost me in the United States to get similar things made. I later learned they were able to accomplish that lower cost because the bronze metal composition was a lower grade and the labor costs were much lower.

We left with a few small samples of bronze sculptures that in our country would have cost five hundred dollars each to have made. Those items, made in their factory, were priced at thirty to forty dollars each. The craftsmanship was not perfect, in that they were reproductions with molds made from other sculptures, but the pricing was extremely low. The catch was that we had to buy hundreds of an individual item to get the cheap price.

We dropped off our young interpreter at her home late that evening. We told her we would see her in the morning for another factory visit in the city.

The next day we went on another plant tour, but it was nearer the city of Hong Kong. We didn't have to ride very far in the cramped car. That time it was to a company which made hand dryers and other electronic parts using a human assembly line. As we viewed a long line of workers sitting in a row, where each person added a small component to the electrical product, I stood with the owner and he told us about his company. I listened with interest as he talked about how many units his people completed each day and bragged about the quality of the dryers.

I finally decided to quiz him but preceded with a little hesitation, "Do you mind if I ask you what you pay each of your workers per hour?"

He replied with a smile on his face, "I pay one dollar per hour with no benefits. Each worker makes eight dollars per day with nothing taken out of his or her paycheck. They are glad to get the money and have a job. It anyone has a complaint, there are hundreds of other people living close to our factory who would love to have their job."

I thought to myself, no wonder all the items produced in China can be manufactured and sent to the United States so cheaply. Even after adding in the cost of the shipping, the products could not possibly be manufactured in our country for anywhere close to the same price.

We left that factory after our visit with a whole new perspective of how the people in China lived and worked. It had been a day full of education. We dropped off our friendly interpreter at her small ground level apartment below one of the large residential buildings and gave her a nice tip. She was appreciative and gave us a big smile as she walked away.

The next day J.R. asked if there was anything else we wanted to do while in China. I thought about it and remembered reading about the ancient terracotta soldiers that had been discovered in recent years somewhere in that country.

I told J.R., "Let's check out where the terracotta soldiers of the first emperor were found and travel there. It should be fascinating to see. I believe they are still in the ground. I read about it recently in the National Geographic Magazine."

He said, "You are right. I've read about that myself, but in all the trips I've made here, I've never taken the time to go see it. Let me check into the details, and we can possibly do that tomorrow."

He was able to set up the trip, and we were to fly to Xian where they were located. It would require a three hour plane flight to the central part of the country, but he told us he thought it would be worth the time.

The next day, after the plane ride, we arrived in Xian and took a taxi directly to the area that included a huge museum. As it turned out, the eight thousand life-size clay soldiers had only been discovered in the early 1990s by a farmer. He had been digging a well in an open field a mile from the huge dirt pyramid which held the first emperor of China from 2,200 years ago. The farmer had dug down around twenty feet and discovered some broken terracotta that was obviously made by humans. As he expanded his hole, he began to find many more pieces.

The area was excavated and widened over a period of years to reveal thousands of those sculptures. They were lined up in formation as if they were going into war and were holding axes, spears and bows with arrows made from ancient bronze. There were also bronze chariots with life-size horses along with other amazing artifacts. Some of the terracotta soldiers were broken and were being put back together, while others were intact.

Immediately, when removed from the ground and exposed to oxygen, the terracotta surface began to lose its colorful paint that would flake and fall away. It was decided that the terracotta had first been covered with a coating of egg yolk to form a base layer, and the colorful paint was then added over that solution. When the paint was exposed to air a couple of thousand years later, it would oxidize and crumble off. After digging up over eight thousand of the soldiers, the decision to stop the excavation was made until scientists could figure out how to avoid the loss of the beautiful paint. They had no idea how many more were still hidden under ground. That trip to see the soldiers turned out to be the highlight of the entire journey to China, and I was extremely glad I had thought about it.

We left the area and the soldiers who stood side by side about twenty feet below ground level. They were all covered by new, heavy metal buildings. We had an increased appreciation of what had been discovered just a few years earlier as we went into the main museum.

The individual who had made the discovery years earlier was sitting inside the museum, and all day long he signed souvenir books with photos of his discovery. He earned five dollars for each signature. I was sure he was now a very wealthy man. He smiled and thanked me as he added his signature to my book.

We walked through another facility selling souvenirs and realized that we could buy reproductions of the soldiers. We were told the cost was $4,000 each for a set of four half-size figures. The cost, if purchased through that location, included shipping them back to our homes in the United States.

Jim and I checked around and were told that a set of four, in half-size, could be bought for around three to four hundred dollars directly from the kiln where they were being reproduced. The catch was that only one company was allowed to ship those out of China. Even the replicas were considered to be valuable antique reproductions by the government, because they were being made at the local kiln out of the same clay from the area which had been used over two thousand years earlier.

We decided to travel a few miles away and visit the actual kiln to see them made and check out if we could buy them cheaper.

It turned out to be an interesting side trip. We watched the dark clay added by hand to the molds where it was later fired in a furnace that was powered by burning coal. We purchased two sets of four soldiers for around three hundred dollars per set and figured we could easily find a way to get them shipped home for a bargain. That didn't turn out to be the case.

We found out later that we had been told correctly that only one company was allowed to ship them out of the country. We had to backtrack to get that company to handle the actual shipping. The shipping was two thousand dollars for both sets, but the overall cost was still cheaper than the original price quoted at the museum. I was sure they would not arrive in one piece after being packaged and shipped on a skid, but the packaging must have been well done, because none of them were harmed when we finally received the sculptures many months later.

That evening J.R. recommended we attend a special dinner with entertainment, based on a brochure he had been given before we left Xian. It was to be at the Tang Dynasty Theater Restaurant and included a formal dinner with many courses, followed by music and dancers on a stage. We decided to do that, and after a fantastic meal the performance was presented in four segments. There were many young women in ornate costumes including masks, large feathers, sequins and silk. All were about the same height, with short dark hair, and looked so similar that we discussed the possibility of them being clones.

As they danced around the stage, we talked about how we had seen very few older Chinese people throughout our trip. We wondered where all the older people were. We guessed the interpreter had been right when she told us a few days earlier that they generally stayed at home and took care of the one child, while the younger generation traveled around the city.

Our next stop was to go back to Beijing for a few days to continue touring that city and see some of the more spectacular sights. Once we arrived, we worked out a tour to The Forbidden

City. That was where the palace was located for the emperors who had ruled China for over seven hundred years. Many different emperors came and went over those years, but all lived within the confines of The Forbidden City.

Currently, that complex served as a large museum. It had been that way for the past one hundred years, since China discontinued having a formal emperor. The architecture was all distinctly Chinese with arched roofs, orange-colored terracotta tiles, and large wooden beams holding up the many buildings and forming the walls. There were various bronze sculptures and vases placed throughout the outer courts and many areas with long stone steps transitioning to different levels.

It was an impressive place, and during all the hundreds of years the different emperors lived there, no one from the outside had been allowed to enter uninvited. We were told that major meetings had been held in special chambers designed for that purpose. We were allowed to visit those areas and also the area where the emperor ate, slept and worked throughout the day. Those places were smaller than I had expected. We even got to see the padded bench where he had sat during major meetings with foreign diplomats. There were elaborately decorated silk screens and artwork placed around the walls.

There was a long line of smaller buildings next door that had housed a large number of women the emperor had used for sexual favors. We were told those were his concubines. It must have been difficult for him to keep up with all of them. Close by, there was also a separate area for worship with wooden floors and an altar. I found it interesting that those two areas were located so close together.

It was enjoyable visiting that historical place. On the day we were there, many individuals crowded around the buildings with cameras taking pictures of the ancient complex. Most seemed to be from China, but many were from other countries. I heard many different languages spoken as I walked among the crowds.

From the Forbidden City, we drove about forty miles west of Beijing to a portion of the Great Wall. We were told that particular spot was a favorite for tourists because it offered parking spaces and restrooms.

Along the way I engaged our male guide and interpreter in conversation, since he spoke very good English.

I first asked, "How do you feel about living in a communist country?"

He responded, "It's not too bad. I grew up here and am used to that form of government and its restrictions. The main problem I see, when comparing myself to others like you from the United States, is that I am not free to create a better life for myself by working hard. No matter how hard I work here, I will still remain at the same level, and all decisions will be made for me by the government."

He went on to explain, "I'm a very motivated person. That's why I have learned to speak many different languages, and the reason the government has allowed me to be an interpreter for tourists. I have personal goals to someday own my own business. I joined the communist party a few years ago, because that's the only way I have a chance of getting ahead of the others in China who are stuck at a low level of existence. Eventually, I want to travel to the United States, go to school and start a company so I can own a home and raise a family there. In China, I am not allowed to do those types of things and be independent."

I found all he had said very interesting. Because he was only around twenty-five years old, I was sure, eventually, his dreams would come true.

When we arrived at our destination, I could immediately see the high mountains and part of the massive Great Wall rising up from where we parked. As I got out of the car and looked around at the mountains, the wall could be seen for miles, as it had been built along the highest ridges. Every quarter of a mile or so there were large structures built on the Great Wall that I later learned were guard stations. Those buildings, and the many steps making up the wall, were colored a dark gray to almost black, because the building material was all handmade bricks that had been fired to nearly a charcoal color. Those bricks, made from dried mud, clay and straw, were each about four times the size of the normal brick we use in America for our houses. It was obvious there were millions and millions of them included in the Great Wall's construction.

J.R., Jim and I went directly to the entrance and started climbing. The guide said he would wait for us at the bottom. After walking only a couple of hundred yards, I realized I was getting tired. The elevation was steeper than expected, and the steps were uneven. Some steps were eight inches high while others were up to a foot tall. That made it difficult to get from one level to the next. We climbed together until we passed the second guard station about a half of a mile up the mountain. Both J.R. and Jim said they were ready to go back down, but I wanted to continue climbing. I figured I would never have another chance to climb the Great Wall, and I wanted to maximize my experience.

I traveled upwards and over the top of the first mountain and then looked back down to the point where I had started. The people were just small spots in the distance. I passed the sixth guard station and then decided it was time to turn around and go back down. From where I was standing, I could see for miles across the mountain tops, and the huge wall continued for as far as I could see.

I noticed it was very tall and wide. At any one location, it was probably forty to fifty feet tall and at least that wide. Always it ran along the highest ridge on the mountain. Where there were guard stations, those areas were even larger, and everything was made of the dark, oversized bricks.

As I descended the steps on my way back to the parking lot, I thought about what I had recently read describing the Great

Wall. It had been built by the Chinese many years ago to form a barrier between northern China and Mongolia. Because China was such a large land mass, the wall had originally extended for close to five thousand miles. When I thought about that number, I remembered that it was almost three thousand miles from the west coast of the United States to the east coast. That would mean that the Great Wall of China's length was almost twice the distance across our entire country. To me that was definitely impressive. I learned that one end of the wall had been built from unfired clay bricks. That part had eroded over the years. Most of the wall made from the fired bricks still stood and looked like it was built recently.

After leaving the Great Wall, we traveled back to Beijing. I began to think about how wonderful an American dinner would taste. The food in China was good, but different. Everything there had its own particular flavor, and I looked forward to enjoying something more familiar.

That evening Jim and I went out to a nice restaurant and ordered chicken. We had noticed at other restaurants we never seemed to get any white meat.   All that we had previously been served was dark meat, so we wondered if they used the white meat for another purpose. At that meal, Jim started out by requesting he be brought some white meat. When it arrived about thirty minutes later we were pleased, but they also brought us boiled chicken feet and the entire chicken's head that had been boiled and mounted on a round stick. The head had been cooked but still contained the reddish comb with open eyes. It was disgusting. As I looked around the restaurant, some of the customers were chewing on the chicken feet, so I guess they also ate the heads.

On our last evening, we ate at Kentucky Fried Chicken. It was similar to one found in the United States. We ordered from photos displayed on the wall above the counter. We got to choose our meal from three different numbered pictures. At least we knew it would be something we were used to eating, so that made us happy. The food was very good. I hoped they had to meet standards established by the franchise.

The next day, we left the hotel and were taken to the airport in a taxi. Along the way, we discussed how Jim had worked things out to have all of his samples and brochures shipped from Beijing directly to his business in Tennessee. The terracotta soldiers we had purchased were to be packaged and sent to us by ship. They were scheduled to arrive a month or two later.

As our flight left the ground in Beijing, I knew I would be traveling for over thirty hours before finally arriving back in Wilmington. It would be very tiring.

I sat in the plane and thought about our trip. I knew it had been worth all the cost and effort to visit that country, so different from ours. Experiencing that culture had been exciting. I also realized I probably would never go back. It was nice to have been able to do it with my younger brother, Jim.

"The secret of genius is to carry the spirit
of the child into old age,
which means never
losing enthusiasm."

Aldous Huxley

Brazil, South America
October 2013

The time I had been anxiously waiting for all year had finally arrived. I was to travel to Porto Alegre, Brazil, so I could participate in the 2013 World Masters Track and Field Championship. I had been competing in Masters Track and Field since 2009 throwing the javelin and shot put. This would be my first world competition outside the United States.

Trent and I began the trip by driving to Raleigh, NC on the morning of October 14th. From Raleigh we flew to Houston.

While sitting at the airport in Houston and waiting for our next flight, I began to think back over the past year, and earlier, to the many events that had led me to this point in time. I had participated in a lot of track meets around the country during 2013, and Trent had competed in most of them by race walking. Those outdoor meets had taken place in South Carolina, Georgia, Virginia, Massachusetts, Ohio, Kansas, Nevada, Utah, and North Carolina. The meets in North Carolina included two in Charlotte, one in Raleigh and others in Wilmington.

Earlier in the year in March, I had competed in the U.S. Indoor Masters National Championships in Landover, MD. Since that meet was indoors, the only event I competed in was the shot put, and I used a special rubber-coated ball to throw on a special gym floor. I finished in third place at that national meet and received a bronze medal. I was satisfied with my outcome because of the large number of competitors and the tough competition.

The reason I mention that particular meet is that an interesting thing happened to me.

Immediately after finishing my last throw in the competition, two ladies walked up and asked, "Are you Edward Hearn?"

I replied, "Yes."

One of them said, "You have been randomly chosen to be drug tested. You are one of 50 masters athletes out of 1,050 here today to be tested. You need to follow us."

I followed them into a special room set up for USADA, the United States of America Anti-Doping Agency, where I was expected to give them a urine sample. I also had to fill out a lot of paperwork.

Their decision to drug test me presented an immediate problem because I had just used the restroom before starting the competition. When I was finally able to give them a small sample, they told me it wasn't enough. I was then given two bottles of water to drink. I was told I couldn't leave until they had enough urine for their tests. I had to drink five bottles of water over two hours before I was able to give them enough. At the end of the test, they told me I would receive the results in a few weeks.

After the samples were taken and everything was in order, I left Maryland in the car with a friend, Joe Sheridan, who had traveled with me to the event. We were determined to get back home to Wilmington that night and were facing a nine hour drive in heavy traffic.

For the first 50 miles, I had to get off interstate I-95 at almost every exit to find a restroom. That irritated Joe, but I was so full of water I couldn't help it. We finally arrived back in Wilmington at 3:00 a.m., and both of us were exhausted.

The drug test results finally arrived five weeks later. They came back negative. There should have been no reason for me to be worried, but USADA took so long to get back to me, I didn't know if there was a problem. When the results arrived in the mail I was relieved, because I really wanted to compete in the upcoming world championship in Brazil.

While still waiting at the Raleigh airport for our plane that was to take us to South America, I thought back to the very beginning of my masters track involvement during July of 2009. I had attended the U.S. Masters National Track and Field Championship held in Oshkosh, Wisconsin. While there, I threw the 5K shot put 41½ feet for a fifth place finish in the nation. I also threw the 600 gram javelin 154 feet for a third place finish. I had just turned 60 years old, so I had entered the five year age bracket of M60-64. I felt that if I could spend some serious time lifting weights at the gym over the winter, I would come back stronger in the spring.

At 64 years old, my best performances had occurred during the U.S. Masters National Track and Field Championship in Berea, Ohio in July of 2011. In the shot put event at that competition, my farthest toss was over 45 feet for a second place finish. I missed first place by only one foot. In the javelin event, I had a throw of almost 170 feet for second place and was only a few feet out of first place.

During the years of 2010, 2011, and 2012, at each of those three major national championships, I threw the javelin over 166 feet. They were my best javelin throws for each season, but I didn't win the national championship any of those years. Finally, in Kansas City in August at the 2013 U.S. Masters National Track and Field Championship, I won the javelin event at age 64 and received a gold medal. My winning throw was 47.84 meters, which was over 156 feet. I was thrilled with the achievement. It finally gave me a national champion title.

During the 2013 regular season, I led the nation in the U.S. Masters national ranking system with the javelin throw I made in Charlotte, four days after pulling my right groin muscle. That throw was 48.75 meters, and it remained my best for the year. Just weeks before the trip to Brazil, I competed in a Nevada meet and had throws of 48.55 meters and 48.57 meters. Those were good throws and had me excited about my potential outcome at the world competition in Brazil.

Trent did very well with her race walking in 2013, and I was very proud of her. She had competed in 1500 meter races, which were just less than one mile, and also 5K races, which were 3.1

miles. Both were tough distances, and she handled them well. Her training throughout the year involved going on long, fast walks in Wilmington. Her practice walks covered 4, 6, 10 and 12 mile outings. Sometimes she even went further, if she had a half marathon or a full marathon coming up in the schedule. Through 2013, I think she completed three full marathons and twelve half marathons. Cool stuff, in my opinion!

During the fall and early spring, I tried to do some of those half marathons with her by speed walking and jogging, but they were hard races at 13.1 miles. I didn't see how she did it, but she was usually faster than me, even though I had done some jogging along the way.

Our layover in Houston finally ended, and we boarded the flight to San Paulo, Brazil. That was our next stop before traveling on to Porto Alegre. The flight lasted all night. Trent and I occupied two of the six pods in the very front of the plane. Those seats were very spacious and easily made into a bed with a blanket and pillow.

We landed in San Paulo where we had a four hour layover. After a three hour flight, we eventually arrived at our final destination. We had been traveling for almost 31 hours.

We were finally in Porto Alegre, Brazil. The city was big with a population of two million. It was filled with tall buildings which we saw in the afternoon sun as our plane landed. We gathered our luggage, including my javelin, and took a cab to our hotel, the Mercere of Manhattan. Our driver could speak no English. We gave him a written note with the address and then sat quietly while he drove like a wild man through the congested traffic. After arriving at the hotel, we changed clothes and put on our USA uniforms and went over to the stadium to be a part of the opening ceremony.

During our drive to the stadium, I remembered a similar trip two years earlier at the World Championships in Sacramento. Trent and I had gathered with the U.S. team and marched into the stadium following the United States banner and flag held at the front of our large group. I thought about that last opening ceremony and was excited about what was to happen.

When we arrived, there were athletes standing everywhere in colorful uniforms waiting for the opening ceremony to begin. We could identify many of the countries represented by the names on the fronts and backs of their uniforms.

I walked over to a tall fellow with a nice green and white uniform and asked him, "Do you speak English?"

He replied, "Sure mate, I speak good English with an accent, and my name is Nick."

I told him, "My name is Ed, and I'm from the United States, North Carolina in particular. I have an accent also, and it is southern."

He thought that was funny and we had a nice conversation.

While we searched for the group of men and women dressed in USA uniforms, I met many interesting people. One in particular was an older lady from the U.S. She told me her name was Johnnyne Vallien, and she was 88 years old. She added that she normally participated in 8 different events. I found that amazing, but then most of the athletes were amazing in their own ways as I got to know them, found out their current ages, and what events they were planning to participate in during the competition.

As it began to get dark, the crowds in the stadium grew. The athletes assembled in groups behind the stadium where large flags on poles representing many different countries were being held by individuals. We found the American flag in the confusion, and as I looked around, I was surprised at how many people from each country had come to the ceremony. In our group from the USA, there were probably only about 150. I had expected many more, but was told that not everyone could arrive in Brazil in time for the opening ceremony.

As the different countries started marching into the stadium, I looked around at the thousands involved. The stadium lighting was not as bright as it should have been, and the jumbotron was brightly lit and stood out in the darkness. Our country's team walked together around the outer track and passed the spectators in the stands. Everyone was waving their country's flags and cheering. We waved at the crowds, many of whom were taking photographs.

As we rounded the track, we passed the main tent in the middle of the field. As each country went by it, a band on stage played a variety of music. After we completed the entire quarter mile track, surrounded by thousands of other athletes, we began to assemble in the middle of the field still grouped by individual countries. Many athletes had small flags they were waving. Everyone was friendly and smiling. We stood for maybe 45 minutes as all the countries finally got in place. The announcer then made a short speech over the loud speaker and repeated it in different languages. The band played music, and everyone interacted with the other athletes standing close by.

Finally Trent, Shaaron Sellars, a track friend from Atlanta, and I decided the celebration would be over soon. We knew we had better beat the crowd to the few large buses outside the stadium if we were to get to our hotels at a reasonable time. Shaaron told us her javelin had not been on the plane when she arrived. She had made several phone calls trying to locate it.

While we sat on the bus talking, a large fireworks display took place in the stadium. Nick, the fellow I had met earlier from Australia, was seated close to me and told us Australia was to host the event in 2016, after France served as host in 2015.

He said, "I hope we add fireworks to our opening ceremony, because it's quite impressive."

After filling the bus with people from the assorted countries, we traveled back through the city three miles to our hotel. We ate a supper of pasta around 10:00, went to our room and quickly fell asleep after anticipating what the next day would hold. The plan was to start at the stadium for a team meeting at 10:30 to get details about the upcoming individual competitions.

I got up the next morning at 6:30 and had a bowl of oatmeal, nuts and strawberries in the room. We were on the ninth floor of the Mercere of Manhattan Hotel, which was a nice place, but the rooms were small. We had a bedroom, a bathroom with a small sink and toilet, plus a tiny shower. In the living room there was a sink, microwave and small refrigerator. We had a small couch and table with two chairs. There was not much additional space. The walls were bare, and the floor was a light-colored artificial wood. There was a television, but only one channel was broadcast in English. We found each night there was an English speaking movie on that channel. We would watch it before falling asleep.

Our biggest surprise was the inefficient bus system put into place to get the thousands of athletes to the stadiums from their various hotels. Four different stadiums were to be used, and they were scattered all over the city. I was to compete in two of them. Because of the problem with the buses, we decided to take a taxi to the main stadium to register. Luckily, we shared the ride with an athlete who spoke both English and Spanish who could communicate with the driver. We gave the driver the written address of the main stadium, but found out later the address from the Internet was wrong. The driver was headed to the middle of the city, in the wrong direction. The fellow with us recognized the error because he had been to the city a day earlier. After some discussion, which I didn't understand, we got turned around and eventually found the correct place. The taxi ride cost $20 because of the detour and was paid in their paper money.

In the afternoon, after visiting the stadium and getting registered, we decided to try the bus system to get back to our room because we had plenty of extra time. That turned out to be a mistake and taught us a lesson. We waited for thirty minutes for the correct one to arrive, which was scheduled to leave the stadium at an exact time, only to find out after we boarded it that we had to wait another hour and a half before it left that location. After that experience, we couldn't imagine trying to depend on their bus system to get us to our scheduled events on time.

I found out my qualifying round for the shot put had been

cancelled for Friday. That would leave all the competitors going directly into the finals on Saturday morning at 8:00. That was fine with me, because the qualifying round would have only made me tired and sore. The competitors who would have been in the qualifying round would first have to be narrowed down to the top 12 from the large number entered. Later, that number would be narrowed to the top eight who would be given three more throws. Those remaining eight individuals in the finals would be competing for the three medals of gold, silver and bronze.

The day before, I talked with a few guys from the U.S. with whom I had competed over the past few years. Those included Doug Torbert, Andy Smith, William Harvey, Fred Monesmith and Richard Watson. Doug had turned 61 years old, and during the last month had broken the all-time American record for the shot put in his age bracket with an outstanding distance of 16.67 meters. That left him just short of the world record, which was set years earlier by a thrower who was disqualified at a later meet for taking performance enhancing drugs in the form of steroids. Doug said his plan was to break his new American record and possibly set a new world record on Saturday. He would easily win the shot put event in our age bracket. I wanted to win a second or third place medal behind Doug, but with the competitive group from around the world I would be throwing against, I was aware that would be tough. If I could get close to my best throw of the 2013 season of 13.66 meters, or 45 feet, I knew I might have a chance.

Later that day, Trent and I toured some of the city. We found a natural history museum in the area and spent a few hours inside. South America is a prime location for dinosaur fossils of the Permian and Triassic eras from 250-300 million years ago. I was interested to see their exhibits.

After that, we went to the stadium where I would be throwing the shot put on Saturday in order to become familiar with how to get there, and also to check out the throwing area. Then we took my shot put and javelin back to the first stadium to have them weighed and checked in. They would be held there and only given back just before the competitions were to take place.

In all the confusion with the number of items they were dealing with, I thought I would be surprised if they got both of my impounded implements to my events on time. The finals were set on Saturday for my shot put at 8:00, and on Tuesday for my javelin at 8:00, at two different stadiums across town.

That evening on our visit to one of the stadiums, SOGIPA, we watched the conclusion of the older men's decathlon involving the pole vaulting event. We watched men from 65 to 84 years old pole vault in different age brackets. It was an amazing thing to see. At the other end of the same stadium, the 65 to 69 year old men were throwing the javelin. One of the men competing, Fred Monesmith from the U.S., had the best throw of the group with a toss of 33 meters. He had recently turned 65 and had moved up to that next age bracket. Fred told me he had only one event in the decathlon left after the javelin, which was the 1500 meter race. After two days of competition, he wasn't looking forward to it because he was already exhausted.

At 10:00 the next morning, we planned to take an open-air bus tour through the city of Porto Alegre. While waiting in the lobby, we ran into another javelin thrower from the USA team. His name was Dick Richardson. I had thrown with him numerous times over the past five years. He had just aged up the past summer to the 65 to 69 age bracket. He told me he had been competing in masters competitions for over fifteen years and had traveled all over the world to attend those events. We discussed upcoming world meets we both hoped to attend, including the World Championship in France in 2015 and the World Championship in Australia in 2016.

I also got into a conversation with a Frenchman using mostly sign language, but we did share some words we both understood. He was 73 years old, and his event was the pole vault. He was small but very strong in his upper body. He told me he had been the national champion of France in the pole vault event for the past 17 years.

During that day, I had conversations with various people from many other countries. Most of them were excited athletes, but one was a military guard at one of the stadiums. He was friendly and tried to communicate with me once he knew I was from the U.S., indicated by the shirt I was wearing. All we were able to understand from each other was that it was a beautiful afternoon and about 75 degrees.

The bus tour around the city was interesting. There were earphones available at each seat. We listened in English about historical features around the large city of Porto Alegre. The buildings varied from 100 year old structures in need of repair to much newer ones. We exited the tour bus at a large building near a waterway that contained numerous market spaces selling meats, vegetables, fruits, and baked goods of all types. It also contained some restaurants, and we entered one and ate a lunch of fried egg, French fries, rice and grilled chicken along with a local soda somewhat similar to ginger ale.

Later we went to our room in the hotel to get some rest so I could prepare for the next day's finals in the men's M60 shot put event. Shaaron Sellars had been with us during the day, and we all had a good time. Sharron's javelin had still not arrived from the U.S., and she had been getting more concerned as the day passed. She kept checking with the airport, but figured by that time the javelin may have been shipped back to Atlanta.

Trent and I had a nice supper and went to bed early because I had to get up at 5:30. The person in charge in the lobby had lined up a taxi for 6:30 in the morning because I needed to be at the stadium by 7:00 to get warmed up. My event was scheduled to be the first of the day. I was sure it would start on time at 8:00.

Trent's race walking event was scheduled at a different stadium from mine. It was scheduled to start at 10:00. She had been having trouble with her calf muscles cramping, so she decided not to race and instead go to my shot put event. I hated that for her because it was her second chance to be a part of a world championship, but it would be fun to have her present to watch the shot put event take place.

After all the athletes from the different countries showed up, we were checked through security and allowed to enter the stadium at 7:15 a.m. We warmed up, stretched and then threw some practice throws for twenty minutes. There were so many participants I only got four practice throws before we started at 8:00.

My first official throw, out of my three attempts, turned out to be my best. I achieved a toss of 13.11 meters, or almost 43 feet. I knew right away it would allow me to move ahead to the finals that included the top twelve competitors. Because we did not have the qualifying round the previous day, the group was to be narrowed to the top twelve competitors after the first three throws, and then to the top eight competitors after three additional throws.

I went into the finals in fifth position, and that was where I finished the competition. My friend, Doug Torbert, who held the American record, easily finished in first place for the gold medal. He did not set a new personal record, even though he won the competition. A man from Switzerland took second place, a man from Poland took third place, a man from Puerto Rico took fourth place and I took fifth. I was happy, even though I didn't win a medal, because I had been having trouble over the last month reaching 13 meters. Two and a half months earlier, I had reached my season best of 13.66 meters, or 45 feet. I was aware I had just been part of a world championship, and I felt good about a fifth place finish in my second best event.

Trent and I then went back to the main stadium, CETE, in a taxi with Shaaron and Doug. Doug talked about his early morning car crash. On the way to the stadium that morning, his driver had gone through a red light, and another car had crashed broadside into them and spun the taxi completely around. Doug was bruised on his left side but was able to catch another taxi to get him to the stadium on time. We had read that many of the drivers in Porto Alegre drove like wild men. It was the reason Trent and I hadn't rented a car. At the stadium that morning, I heard another story about an athlete whose taxi driver had hit a pedestrian.

As required, Doug and I had checked in our shot puts at the main stadium a few days earlier. They were supposed to be waiting for us at the time of our event. None of the checked shot puts ever arrived, and we had to use furnished implements we were unfamiliar with for the competition. For me it wasn't a big deal, and Doug had been able to win using them, but I was concerned as to whether my special javelin would show up by 8:00 on Tuesday morning for the qualifying round at a different stadium. I was sure the few furnished javelins would not include an 80 meter like mine. I decided I would just have to wait to see what happened because it was out of my control.

After Doug and I arrived back at the main CETE stadium, we checked on our missing shot puts and were told they didn't know where they were. Finally, after 4:00 that afternoon, they showed up with no explanation of where they had been all day. Because of the language barrier it was very hard to communicate, and there was a lot of all-around confusion.

Trent and I made a point to attend Doug's shot put award ceremony where they displayed the three flags of the winning countries. He and the two other medal winners stood on the podium as the American anthem was played. Each competitor received his medal as it was placed around his neck while the cameras clicked. For the other top finishers, there were certificates of achievement, called diplomas, and I received one for my fifth place finish. Afterward, we met up with Shaaron, Doug and John Wirtz from the U.S. for a nice supper at a fancy restaurant. We talked about the day's happenings and about our earlier college "glory days" in track and field.

The next day was an "off day" for competition so Shaaron,

Doug, Trent and I planned an eight hour tour to a couple of vine-yards. We gathered at 8:00 in the morning for the scheduled bus trip that would start with a two hour's drive to the first vineyard. That seemed like a nice way to spend a quiet Sunday. Shaaron let us know her javelin had finally arrived, and she was happy.

At 10:00 our bus arrived at the first vineyard which was in a very hilly area. It was much cooler there because of the high altitude. The hillsides were covered with long, green rows of manicured grapevines. There were 25 people on the tour. As we entered the main building, the tour guide explained how the wine was made, all the way from harvesting the grapes to filling the bottles. We sampled five different wines including two reds, a rose and then two white sparkling wines. That vineyard, named the Casa Valduga, was famous for its sparkling wines, which were very good. I thought the first three wines offered were also especially nice.

During the wine tour, I began to feel mellow and quite relaxed. It didn't take too many glasses to get in that condition, so I decided I had better slow down. The highlight of the visit was lunch. We entered a large room with a long table in the center with flowers, fine china and silver. There were place settings for all of us. To either side of the table were huge oak casts turned on their sides so we could view the lined up circular ends.

The atmosphere of the place was really nice, and the variety of food that was served for the meal was fantastic. We started with two varieties of salad greens and then a warm bowl of soup. That was tasty. We were then individually served many more items including breads, pastas, chicken, beef, cheeses and items of which I wasn't sure of the names. I became full fairly quickly as we were offered additional platters of the wonderful food.

Suddenly, down the long table, an individual eating with us started singing. I could tell by the quality of his voice he was a professional opera singer. I found out later he was just visiting the vineyard like the rest of us and had not been hired for the occasion. While we ate, he sang a total of four songs. His singing was a complete surprise. When he finished, we all stood and applauded. In talking with him afterwards, he told us his name was Giovanti. He had made the meal highly unusual and very enjoyable.

We left the first vineyard and stopped shortly thereafter at the second. I found a shady spot on the lawn in green clover and stretched out flat on the ground. The temperature was 80 degrees. It was so pleasant, I didn't go inside for the tour. We were there for an hour before boarding the bus for the long drive back to the city. We arrived at our hotel at 7:30 in the evening.

Trent and I went immediately to our room on the ninth floor, ate a light supper from our own refrigerator, and drifted off to sleep while watching television. Shaaron had two events the following day, and we planned to attend and cheer for her.

Monday, for me, was supposed to be a day to relax and enjoy the competition of others. The morning started off with several hours of heavy rain. We stayed in the room and got to the main stadium late because we thought those events originally scheduled for the morning would be postponed.

We found there had been only slight delays in the competitions in spite of the heavy rain. Most of the events had taken place on schedule, even with an electrical storm taking place. Shaaron's event for the morning had been the triple jump, and she placed seventh. She told us one lady competing had slipped on the wet runway and had broken her leg. That was a tragic accident. Most athletes had been surprised the competition continued during the rain.

I went back to the main stadium to check on my javelin that I would need for my qualifying round the next morning. The man in charge assured me it would be delivered during the night to the correct place. Because my shot put had not made it to the stadium a few days earlier, I was still concerned.

Later in the afternoon, Trent and I traveled to the ESEF stadium to watch Shaaron participate in the qualifying round for the women's discus throw. She had some good throws, but out of 30 participants, she didn't make the final 12. During the day, I talked and made friends with numerous athletes from many countries, including others from the U.S. and South Africa.

On the morning of my qualifying round for the javelin event, I woke up at 5:30. I got ready for my 8:00 start that would take place in the beautiful SOGIPA stadium. That stadium was older than the others, but in very good condition. On either end were large, concrete entrance columns that resembled something that could be seen at an Olympic stadium. Those columns had large Olympic overlapping circles in five different colors over one entranceway. That made me believe the location had been used for part of the summer Olympic Games at some point in the past.

I communicated the best I could with the other athletes as we assembled in a large group. I met the two athletes from Finland, who I knew would be tough competitors, Bill Pearson from Canada, others from Germany, Peru and additional countries. There were also two others from the United States throwing in my age bracket.

After a few practice throws, I took a moment to notice the cloudless blue sky and the rising sun. It was a gorgeous morning, but I could tell the wind was about to pick up. Because that morning was only to be the qualifying round, I didn't want to get too tired or sore before the final round competition scheduled later in the week. My plan was to get one long throw early on and then pass on the rest of my throws after I was assured of making the finals.

Surprisingly, we were called together right before the start and told everything had changed. We would be competing not only in the qualifying round that morning, but also in the finals, which would take place immediately afterwards. Quickly, I assessed how I was feeling physically, and determined it would be a good decision for me, even though I wasn't mentally prepared for the finals to take place that morning.

The competition started soon afterward. I had to first make it into the top eight in order to get the three final throws. Because of the way they had decided to do it, everyone would go into the finals automatically. Normally, I would first have to make it into the top twelve to advance to the next stage. My position in the order was number 19 and there were 23 in my event. Each individual throw was measured and tabulated before the next person could throw, so there were long periods of time when I had to stay pumped up and warm until my time in the rotation came up again.

I wanted to get a good throw at the start while my adrenalin was pumping. Then I would know I could relax and go for my maximum distance on later throws. I started off with an average throw that put me in the final eight for the finals, but I knew I had to do better. During the first round there were throws farther than mine, so the pressure was on me. My second throw was again average. I knew inside I could do better. The Finnish and German competitors had really good throws by the time my third throw was to take place.

On my third throw, I really gave it my maximum effort. I immediately knew from the speed of my body down the runway, the solid plant of my left leg and the swift snap of my arm and wrist I had a good throw as soon as it left my hand. As I looked in the air, the javelin was sailing flat and rising, with the point up. I knew with the power I had put behind it, the throw would be a good one. As it hit the ground, I raised both arms into the air and jumped for joy. I watched the officials measure the distance and when the number came back, I had a mark over 47 meters. At that time, I knew I had a real chance get one of the three medals.

The competition continued and the best Finnish athlete, who was ranked for 2013 as the top thrower in the world for our age bracket, threw 49.50 meters. I knew I would have to get one of my best throws to win. I also had four or five throwers very close in distance right behind me who were all capable of passing my mark.

As it turned out, the top Finnish athlete and I finished the competition in the same order as our earlier throws. I had nailed down second place and was behind the winner by two meters. I was ahead of the third place finisher, another Finnish athlete, by two meters. The number three and number four finishers were only separated by .01 of a meter, or approximately one-fourth of an inch. That was definitely not much when we were throwing close to 165 feet.

Interestingly, the two men from Finland had expected to finish in the number one and two positions. I had been told that information before the competition by a friend who had heard them talking.

I knew that in Finland, the javelin event had always been a focus of national pride. The country handled the event the way the U.S. does with its young athletes in baseball or football. In Finland, the talented boys were selected early, and then they were coached as they got older to push the very best to later success.

For years, and ever since I began throwing 45 years ago in college, Finland had always had some of the top javelin throwers in the world. In the competition that day, I had separated the two Finnish men and forced one of them to take a third place finish. I was pleased with that accomplishment.

In the late afternoon, a few of us went to the "Z Café" to celebrate. Three of our friends would be leaving early in the morning, and we wanted time to talk about the events of the last few days. We had a wonderful time together during supper. I began to settle down, realizing that for me the competition was over, and I had done well.

My fifth place finish in the shot put and my second place finish in the javelin were satisfying. I felt a true sense of accomplishment as I sat back and reflected. Two years earlier in 2011, at my last World Masters Track and Field Championship held in Sacramento CA, I had finished tenth in my age bracket in the shot put and sixth in the javelin.

I got up early the next day expecting to travel to the main stadium to pick up my javelin, take some photos and watch some of the other events. Instead, I was reminded that it was another day of rest, like Sunday, with no competitions taking place. That was good because there were thunderstorms most of the day. Our electricity in the hotel had even been going off and on. During the middle part of the afternoon, I realized how tired I was and slept for two hours. I felt much better afterwards. There was almost nothing on television in English, and after a week it was beginning to get old trying to watch without knowing what was being said.

It was such a messy day we didn't even want to go sight-seeing. We just ate sandwiches in the room for supper. Already a bunch of other competitors were on their way home. We were not leaving until Friday. My award ceremony for the javelin was scheduled for the following morning when I would receive my silver medal. I was definitely looking forward to it.

The next morning the rain and storms of the previous day were gone. The sky was clear and the sun appeared. My goal for the day was to enjoy the award ceremony, pick up my silver medal and pick up my javelin that should have been returned to the main stadium. Many of the competitors were now finished and were picking up their equipment. I didn't want someone to take my javelin in the confusion. The one javelin I brought on the trip cost $1,200.

As we left the hotel, we were pleasantly surprised the correct bus was stopped outside waiting to pick up athletes. That bus took us directly to the stadium we were trying to get to. I went over to the implement holding room and happily found my javelin waiting in a corner. Vidal, who helped me, asked if I would consider trading him the top of my USA uniform for a Brazil uniform top he owned. I told him I would do it because everyone seemed to be trading parts of their uniforms for other country's outfits. Shaaron had already traded a nice USA warm-up jacket for a South Africa jacket. I told Vidal I still had to get my picture taken in the USA uniform during the awards ceremony, and we could make the exchange when I picked up my javelin in the afternoon. He seemed happy. He told me he would watch my javelin so it wouldn't disappear.

I then went off to watch the ladies' javelin throw event. A lady from Canada, named Barb, who I had first met in New Brunswick, Canada during the fall, would be throwing in the 55 to 59 age bracket. She ended up winning and set a new Canadian record for her age bracket of 37 meters.

Next, Shaaron was to throw the javelin in the 50 to 54 age bracket. She was throwing her javelin that had finally arrived from the airport, which I had painted for her in five different colors earlier in the spring. It was beautiful. After her first three throws, she signaled to us she had made it to the finals where she would get an additional three attempts. Shaaron ended up getting her farthest toss of the year at nearly 25 meters and placed number six in the competition. She was really excited, and Trent and I were glad for her.

I found out my award ceremony would not take place until after four o'clock in the afternoon. Trent and I left the stadium to briefly return to our hotel room. I wanted to get an extra shirt, so I could go ahead and swap with Vidal for his Brazil uniform top. We arrived back at the stadium around 2:00. I immediately went to pick up my javelin and swap the shirt. Vidal was all smiles. He gave me a bright yellow and green Brazil uniform top with a big Brazil logo on the front. He told me he planned to frame the USA top I had just given him. I thought that was pretty cool.

My awards ceremony finally took place shortly after 4:00. I met up with my two Finnish competitors. We communicated the best we could. While waiting to take our places on the award podium, Shaaron handed me a small American flag. Upon seeing it, the large group of spectators from Finland handed both of the other competitors small flags from Finland for them to wave on the podium.

We stepped up on the three platforms of the podium, and the announcer gave the crowd our name, country represented, event and the place in which we had finished in the competition. Behind us, on large individual television screens, our country's flags were displayed, and the Finnish national anthem was played for the winner. Both of the Finnish competitors waved their flags throughout the ceremony. I held the American flag where it could be seen and remained respectful. The medals were placed around our necks as friends took photos and cheered. It was really nice!

After leaving the platform, a whole group of Finnish athletes came up to congratulate me for my second place finish. I believe everyone in that group was a javelin thrower in a different age bracket. Among them I recognized Esu, who held the world record in two different age brackets in the javelin event. I had thrown against him two years earlier at the world championships in Sacramento before he turned 65. He walked over and shook my hand with a big smile on his face while saying something positive in his language. I knew he remembered me. I thought about the fact I would again be throwing against him when I turned 65 the next year.

Later that evening, after taking a lot of photos at the CETE stadium, Trent and I met Shaaron for a final meal at a nice restaurant. We would be leaving the city the next morning on our long flights taking us back home.

All-in-all, the trip was an enjoyable, fantastic success. I was sure the memories of those last eleven days would remain with me for many years into the future.

*"We read books to find out who we are.
What other people, real or imaginary,
do and think and feel is an essential guide to our
understanding of what we ourselves are
and may become."*

Ursula Le Guin

Back to South Africa
June 2014

I really enjoyed my first hunting trip to South Africa with my brother, Jim, in 2010. We experienced two weeks of excitement and successful hunting. I wanted to do it again, this time with my younger son, Matt. Jim and three of his close friends, Doug Roberts, Gary Wood, and Bob Bible, became part of the 2014 trip along with Matt and me. Doug, Gary and Jim planned to hunt while Bob, Matt and I decided to be observers. My role was to again keep a diary of each day's happenings and take a variety of photographs. By doing that, we could later remember the trip with a detailed, written story and photos.

I was originally scheduled to fly to Atlanta on a small commuter plane around noon. However, because of impending bad weather in Wilmington, I took the only large plane and had to leave at 7:00 that morning. That way I was sure to make it, so I could meet up with my son and the others. As a result, I waited at the airport in Atlanta for many hours until the rest of the group showed up at 3:00. They had driven by car from Nashville.

While later sitting on the plane in Atlanta at 7:55 p.m., waiting for take-off for our fifteen hour flight to Johannesburg, South Africa, I re-read my diary from my first trip to Africa in 2010 where I talked about how exhausted I had been after finally arriving in Africa. I was sure the upcoming trip would be the same.

Just a week earlier, I had received an email from Jim telling me the outfitter for our trip advised us to get malaria pills. I hadn't even thought about that need, because on our last trip to South Africa malaria had not been an issue in the area we hunted. On this trip, we would be driving northwest of Johannesburg for four hours and would be entering malaria country. We would be 80 miles from Botswana, in the northern part of South Africa.

I spent most of the next day trying to obtain a prescription. My personal doctor had been off work for the day, and no one else had been willing to write a simple prescription until I forced the issue. I started taking the pills two days before leaving town. My instructions were to take one each day while on the trip and then one each day for seven days afterward. As I later found out, only three people on the trip had decided to take the malaria medicine.

I was excited because my thirty year old son, Matt, was on the trip with me. His older brother, John, had been invited, but he couldn't work it out because of commitments at work and home. I was sure the trip would be a "once-in-a-lifetime" positive experience for Matt, and he would come away feeling good about our time together. Matt purchased a bunch of supplies and clothes especially for the trip. I had bought him a pair of binoculars as a Christmas present. He told me he had been practicing with them in his backyard by sighting deer to simulate the African animals.

Finally, we boarded the plane, but before we had taxied down the runway, it was announced there was an issue with the passport of one of the passengers on the plane and that person had to get off. The announcement continued and said the plane couldn't take off until that person's checked and stored bags were removed. Just as the airport workmen started to sort through the luggage already loaded in the underside of the plane, it started raining very hard. That was followed by continuous lightning strikes. The crew stopped sorting the luggage to wait for the weather to get better. We ended up sitting on the plane for three and a half hours at the terminal because of the luggage issue before we started our fifteen hour trip. I got tired just sitting and thinking about the long, upcoming trip in the air.

At 4:00 in the afternoon the next day, we had been in the air, mostly over the Atlantic Ocean, for twelve hours. We still had three hours left before landing in Johannesburg. The flight from Atlanta spanned fifteen hours while traveling east with the trade winds. I was told we would be in the air sixteen hours on the return trip because we would be flying against the winds.

During the flight, I tried hard to go to sleep, but otherwise I read part of a book, watched a movie on a small personal television screen and talked to my neighbor. When I opened my window cover, all I saw were the bright blue skies of daylight, white billowing clouds and plenty of ocean far below. Excitement was building. We were scheduled to land as the sun was going down. I knew it would probably take a few days for my body to get readjusted to the new time. At least we would be in Africa and starting our adventure.

Everyone was exhausted when we arrived after dark around 8:00 in the evening. As I stepped into the terminal, I noticed a gentleman holding a small sign with my name on it in bold letters. It wasn't clear what was happening, because I knew they weren't waiting for me with a car. I approached the man and asked him what the sign was all about. He said he had been told to notify me my duffle bag was still in the Atlanta airport. I didn't know what to say. I knew our group would be leaving quickly and driving to our remote destination four hours to the north. I didn't understand. After having arrived early in Atlanta from Wilmington, I thought the airline should have had plenty of time to get my bag on the plane. I was told to go to the baggage office and tell them my bag had not arrived. By doing that, arrangements for its delivery could be made.

I walked over and presented my baggage claim ticket. An employee at the counter entered that information into the computer. He then promised me my bag would arrive on the next Delta flight from Atlanta at 5:00 the following afternoon. He told me someone would be scheduled to drive it to me at the location where we would be hunting. I thought to myself, if they were able to find us, I would surely be surprised. Luckily, I had packed a few extra clothes in my carry-on backpack. I would probably be fine until my lost bag was delivered. Before leaving the airport, I found a store and purchased toothpaste, a toothbrush, perspiration spray, mouthwash, shaving cream and a razor. I was told I could spend up to $50 per day, and the money would be refunded to me later. I knew that would be the only store I'd be near for the rest of the trip.

After arriving at the lodge, we were able to wind down a little and have a nice meal. Within two hours, we went to bed. I think we all slept like rocks and didn't get up for breakfast until 9:30. Breakfast was outstanding with eggs, bacon, sausage, bread, jam, cereal, yogurt, orange juice and fruit. Everything about the lodge was first-class. The employees were all very nice, including our personal hunter and host, Rassie, and Verwey, another personal hunter.

The first thing we did after breakfast was to drive to a make-shift firing range so everyone could sight-in their rifles. Matt was able to fire Jim's rifle at the firing range and shot three almost perfect shots into the bull's eye of a printed target at fifty yards. I think he immediately liked the experience. The rifle he was using was outfitted with a nice, high powered scope.

On our first day of hunting, everyone left the lodge in two separate trucks, both with open seating in the back. I rode with Matt, who drove, while Doug and Verwey stood in the open back and gave directions. We traveled down dusty roads. The two vehicles split up in order to search different areas on either side of a large road running through the middle of the property. The owner of the lodge had access to 4,500 acres of land where we would be hunting. It was broken into two sections and owned by two different individuals who worked together. Each large piece of land was separated by a main road that ran through the middle with its own entry gate.

Throughout the day, we slowly drove around, looking constantly through the thick undergrowth for movement. Whenever an animal was spotted, it quickly disappeared from the dirt road into the bushes. We saw a variety of African animals including kudus, impalas, red hartebeests, warthogs, vervet monkeys, giraffes and zebras, but they didn't stay around long. Along the way, Doug and Verwey got out of our truck a few times to track a sighted impala, but never got close enough to take a shot.

When we met up at the lodge with those from the other vehicle, I was pleased to hear they had seen many more animals than we had. The property they had searched had much more open land. Our group decided that was where we would hunt the next day. It turned out Gary, who had hunted out of the other vehicle, had wounded a blue wildebeest that disappeared in the thick vegetation after being hit. Because of that, both vehicles would start out by going to that area the next morning to see if we could find the animal.

Sunday morning, I decided to quit taking my malaria pills. We were hunting in the extreme northern part of South Africa during their wintertime. I was told we wouldn't have a problem with mosquitos that time of the year.

We were up for breakfast at 6:00, so we could start searching for animals as the air began to warm. The temperature started out in the low 50s. It was supposed to warm up to the low 70s by noon. I took my medium weight coat off at 10:00, but left on the other layers I was wearing to stay comfortable.

Both vehicles began the hunt on the far side of the main road that ran through the property. On that side, the vegetation was not as thick, so there was a chance to see more animals. We stopped for photographs when we passed a group of eight giraffes standing behind a cluster of trees. They were large with long necks and long legs allowing them to raise their heads up to peer at us through the leaves. The darker patterns on their fur stood out beautifully in the morning sun. They were less afraid of us than the other animals and seemed to mostly be curious, as we stopped and watched. We searched for the wounded blue wildebeest Gary had shot the day before, but never found it.

While we were driving around, we saw small groups of

impalas that quickly disappeared. We saw warthogs with their babies. The mother warthog would always run away with her long, thin tail held high in the air. There was a black-backed jackal that ran across the road right in front of us. The most unusual sighting was a male and female waterbuck. The waterbucks were large animals and the female had no horns. The male we saw had horns that were not typical for the species. Instead of the horns angling upward off the head, they flared directly outward and back on each side. Both horns were probably two feet in length.

We saw three different groups of blue wildebeests. They moved into the dense vegetation as we approached, but were slow to disappear. Verwey told us they must have known we were not hunting for them. He laughed and said that on the next day, if one of us decided to harvest a blue wildebeest, he was sure we would have trouble finding one.

A couple of times that morning, we spotted a male impala that would make a nice trophy mount. Doug left the truck with Verwey to try and get a shot off at the edge of the thick vegetation. On both occasions, he was unsuccessful in getting close enough for a good shot. Doug was focused on shooting an impala. I knew it would happen in the next few days.

During the previous evening, Matt and I had a discussion about the hunting trip. He told me he had changed his mind about just being an observer and wanted to hunt for a zebra. At first I thought he wanted to have a rug made from the beautiful skin, but he explained he wanted to have the head and shoulders mounted as a trophy to remember the trip. I had no problem with that, but told him he needed to be sure he was comfortable with killing the animal for that purpose. I felt sure if he did shoot a zebra, there would be people who would give him a hard time for killing the large animal. Others would think it was fine and congratulate him on the accomplishment. Also, in the area we were hunting, it would not be easy to kill a specific species and the focused hunts were quite involved.

At 1:00 we finished lunch, and everyone took a break at the lodge. The lodge was a medium-sized building with red brick sides and a tiled roof. There were four bedrooms with two beds per room, an owner's suite, a kitchen and a large room with a bar and fireplace where we ate. On the walls of that room there were mounted heads of a large variety of the animals found in the area. Many animal skin rugs were on the floor.

Beside the lodge was a beautiful large pond spanning a couple of acres filled with reeds and clear water. There were a variety of ducks swimming on its surface, including coots and other species I couldn't identify. On the previous day, when we arrived back from our evening outing, there was a large male, horned water-buck standing on the far side of the pond. It quickly disappeared into the woods after we showed up and started watching it.

I was told that a courier was coming sometime during the afternoon to bring my missing luggage. From the airport, it was a four hour drive over many back roads, so I would be amazed if it arrived considering how difficult the place would be to find. I knew I would be glad if it showed up, so I could change clothes and have access to other items I had brought for the trip. It did arrive much later in the day. The courier told us it had taken him 7 hours to find us.

We got up early Monday morning so we could eat breakfast at 6:30 and be in the vehicles by 7:00. The morning was cold and required gloves and extra shirts for warmth. The sky was clear, and the early morning sun began to warm everything very fast. Again in our vehicle, as had been for the past two days, were Verwey, Doug, Matt and myself. We stopped and picked up a black African man at his residence along the way, so there were five in total. Jim's vehicle included Rassie, Bob and Gary, along with him and a black helper they picked up.

After leaving the lodge, we didn't see them again until lunch. At that time, we shared stories of our morning's experiences. Doug had tracked through the brush, on two different occasions, in search of the elusive male impala. Neither time had he been able to get a clean shot, because the group of impalas he sighted had quickly disappeared.

Afterwards, we drove down a dusty, red dirt road splitting the underbrush. We spotted ahead of us three male impalas only two hundred yards away. Doug and Matt were standing in the open back of the truck and leaning against the cab. There was a sand bag lying on top of the cab. Verwey instructed Doug to quickly position his high-power, scoped rifle on the sandbag and take a shot. Doug was after a nice male impala with a large set of horns. He knew this opportunity could be his chance to get one. Before I knew it, he fired his gun. There was a loud noise, and in the distance I could see the impala was hit. It jumped and ran into a thicket where about ten other impalas had been hiding. They all began to run and jump in many different directions. Everyone got out of the truck and started walking down the road to the spot where the animal had been hit. After searching for an entire hour, we could not find the wounded impala. It had run through large thickets of heavy vegetation and disappeared, even though it was obviously injured.

Later, as we were slowly driving down another small road, we spotted a large giraffe. Near it were ten zebras moving slowly away from us while mostly hidden by the vegetation. Verwey and Matt got out and started easing in the direction of the zebras that quickly moved out of sight. I waited in the truck and hoped I would soon hear a shot indicating that Matt might have downed one. After thirty minutes, I saw Verwey and Matt coming back to the vehicle. They explained the group of zebras had moved away from them too fast to catch. The rest of the day was spent driving slowly over level land looking everywhere for animals. Every time we spotted something of interest, it seemed to quickly vanish into the undergrowth.

The next morning, after a good breakfast, we boarded our vehicle at 6:30, again with Verwey. Jim decided to get in our truck, and Doug went to the other one, so the three Hearns could hunt together. The goal was to get in the field at first light, but we ran into a snag as the main gate leading to the property on the other side of the road was locked. The man in charge of that gate had not been told to be there before 7:00 with the key. He finally showed up and opened the gate, and we went on our way.

At 7:40, Jim noticed a huge male kudu standing perfectly still. It was looking into the morning sun while facing us head on from the brush. I saw the animal as Jim set up for the shot, but I was sure, from the distance, it was a female without horns. Verwey looked through his binoculars and confirmed it was a nice, mature male with white horn tips that faced toward us at the very top, indicating a big trophy animal. Jim took the shot at 75 yards from the open back of the truck and dropped the animal. We rushed over to see the kudu and were immediately amazed at the length of its horns. Later, they were measured at 50" in length with plenty of spread between the top of the horns. Its fur was in perfect shape, and the colors and light striping on its back were beautiful. Verwey set up the animal for some quick photos in the early morning light. The animal was then loaded and taken to the skinner's shop a few miles away.

An hour after we left the skinner's shop, we started hunting again from the truck. Within a mile, a group of ten zebras were seen through the thick bushes. Verwey and Matt quickly exited with the rifle and shooting tripod to try and sneak up for a close shot. Everyone else stayed with the vehicle, so as to not scare the animals. Verwey planned to set up the shooting tripod for Matt, and let Matt focus in through the scope to take a shot. After twenty minutes, I heard a shot that must have been at least 500 yards away from us. We couldn't see anything, so we just waited with anticipation for a sign from Verwey for us to advance. Finally, Verwey showed up and said he was sure Matt had hit the zebra with a good shot, but it didn't go down immediately. He needed us to help search for the wounded animal. We followed him to where Matt was waiting, and we began the hunt for the zebra.

After looking for over an hour and not finding the animal in the dense vegetation, we decided to get out of the hot sun and go back to the lodge for lunch. Afterwards, we quickly returned to the area for another hour of searching. We finally gave up and decided maybe the animal had only been injured, and we might find it with the rest of the small herd the next day. We found from that experience the zebra was a tough animal. It didn't go down easily.

Jim decided he would try to find a nice male impala before sunset, so we drove down the dusty roads in search of one. A few were sighted, and Jim left the truck with Verwey a couple of different times, but had no success. The impalas moved away quickly when they saw them coming.

Shortly, before it got dark and the sun was very low in the sky, Jim spotted a male impala at 150 yards. He asked Verwey's permission to take the shot. After approval, he quickly downed the impala where it had stood. We rushed over to take photos and measure the horns. It was a nice trophy impala with 21" horns. We loaded it and later dropped it off at the skinner's shop just as the sun disappeared over the horizon.

As it turned out, earlier in the afternoon, Gary had killed a very nice male impala that had been taken to the skinner's shop. Its horns measured 22 ¾" in length. It was definitely a trophy mount for him. I knew he would be happy because he already had a warthog from the previous day and now the impala. Jim had a super nice waterbuck from the day before with citation-grade horns of over 29", which was almost a record. Plus, he had killed an amazing 50" horned kudu that morning and now the additional 21" horned male impala.

Doug hadn't gotten his male impala, but we expected that to happen the next day. Matt had wounded his zebra, or killed it, and we hoped to find it also.

During the evening, I was told Gary Wood had shot and killed a zebra. He was feeling good about the accomplishment.

Bob Bible had been driving the other vehicle for the past few days and had taken all kinds of kidding from the group. He had planned to be an observer just like me, but said he had earned his "P.H.D." That designation, according to Bob, stood for "Professional Hunter's Driver." He had been driving the truck consistently and doing a good job.

We started early on Wednesday morning at 6:15. It wasn't quite as cold that morning as it had been the first few days. Jim spotted three beautiful oryx, also named gemsbok, on a hillside 200 yards from us, and immediately decided one of them would be his trophy. The truck was stopped, and he sighted from the open bed in the back. That angle gave him a raised view. It wasn't long before I heard his shot. The noise was deafening. We all started walking toward where the animal had been standing behind scattered clumps of thorny bushes. David, our helper, located the place the animal had been and started tracking a blood trail through the foot tall grass. The grass was cream colored and allowed the blood drops to be easily seen.

About fifty yards away, the oryx was found under a small tree where it had fallen and died. After taking multiple photos of that beautifully marked and colorful animal, it was loaded on the back of our vehicle with an electric wench. Our next plan was to stop by the skinner's shop a few miles away. We decided to hunt along the way.

Within a half hour of driving slowly toward the skinner's shop, Verwey noticed a few zebras off in the distance. Since Matt was still after a nice zebra for a head and shoulder mount, he and Verwey jumped from the vehicle with the tripod sticks and the rifle. They walked toward the zebras, while keeping low and hidden behind a mass of seven foot tall, thick bushes. Everyone else stayed behind and waited to hear a shot. Within twenty minutes, we heard it. We waited, wondering what had happened.

After another thirty minutes, Verwey showed up and said we needed to follow him to help search for the zebra. He told us Matt had hit it perfectly, but it ran through the bushes. We noticed blood spots on the red clay and cream colored grass and began to track the zebra. On and on we went, following a blood trail toward the morning sun. We must have walked three-fourths of a mile or farther before we finally found the downed animal. Matt's face lit up with a very big smile, as he looked at me while standing next to the zebra. I was very proud and told him he had just enjoyed the "whole experience" of the hunt.

Before that success, Matt had gone on multiple trips with Verwey into the bush to track different sighted zebras with no positive results. On this occasion, he had shot the zebra and then tracked the wounded animal by following a blood trail. The tracking had covered a long distance, through thick vegetation, to ultimately locate the animal.

When we found the zebra, it was a long distance from the dirt road. Verwey and David had to backtrack all the way to the truck and drive it around thick thorn bushes and trees. By that time it was 10:30 in the morning. They used the electric wench on the truck to load the large animal. That was not before we took a lot of photos of "the great white hunter," Matt, with his trophy zebra. After dropping off the zebra with the skinner, we went to the lodge for lunch and a rest.

At 2:00, Verwey said it was time to head out again. Jim decided he wanted to take a zebra for himself. It wasn't long before one was sighted standing broadside in the dusty road approximately 330 yards ahead of us. Verwey told Jim to wait for the shot until we could get closer, but Jim felt sure his rifle would hit the target accurately based on his earlier target practice from that distance. When Jim fired from the outside cab of the vehicle, I could see the zebra in the distance almost fall, but it jumped up and disappeared in the bush. We drove forward to the spot where the zebra had been standing, but there was no blood or any sign it had been hit. We spent the next hour searching for a blood trail, or a sign of the zebra, without success.

We went back to the truck, and Verwey decided to drive around the area and see if the zebra might be found in a small herd with some others. We searched for an hour and finally spotted a few zebras off in the distance. Jim and Verwey left us and disappeared through the thick bush to see if one of them was the injured animal. Within twenty minutes, we heard a loud shot. Then five minutes later, another shot. Verwey yelled for us to come over. When we arrived, the zebra was on the ground. Jim explained to me they had followed a herd of ten zebras, and the injured one he had shot earlier was limping along behind, having trouble keeping up. After setting up the zebra and taking photos, we loaded it with the wench and drove over to the skinner to drop it off.

The day had consisted of an oryx taken in the early morning, Matt's zebra involving a long hunt, and Jim's wounded zebra trailing the herd. On the return trip to the lodge, Jim also shot a black-backed jackal the size of a medium dog.

As I talked with Verwey in the vehicle on our way back to the lodge, he said "I've had enough zebra action for today. Maybe more tomorrow, but for today with Matt, I've had the longest blood trail search I've ever experienced. Then, we found the injured zebra Jim had wounded, that I thought we would never find."

During the day, in the other truck with Bob and Rassie, Gary had shot an oryx. It had been taken to the skinner's shop about lunchtime. Doug had stayed at the lodge because he wasn't feeling well.

Wednesday night we knew we still had two more days of hunting. We were told an African taxidermist was coming by the lodge to meet with us on Friday. On Saturday we planned to make a trip to his taxidermy studio and then to a curio shop in Johannesburg to purchase some souvenirs before our long flight back home Saturday night.

On Thursday morning, everyone was up by 5:45, and we enjoyed a lite breakfast of pancakes, homemade bread, cereal, yogurt and fruit juice. By 6:20, we started out from the lodge to begin our hunt before sunrise. Our first stop was at the rifle range, so Doug could again test his gun and scope while resting it on the tripod sighting sticks. He took two shots from 50 yards and both were nearly perfect into the bullseye. With his renewed confidence, we started moving slowly in search of game.

The first thing we sighted was a group of impalas in a small clearing. The truck was stopped as the animals moved into the underbrush. Doug and Verwey got out and headed through the vegetation in the direction of the herd. After twenty minutes they returned, and we were off again down the road. They had not found the impalas.

The next thing we saw was a tree full of vervet monkeys. There must have been twenty of the frisky creatures scampering in all directions, as they jumped from the large tree to the ground. Jim had shown interest in taking one of those monkeys for a mount, but completely missed his first shot, as he tried to just graze one of them. He was afraid if he hit it solidly with the high powered bullet, it would tear up the small animal too much for mounting.

We saw a variety of animals including seven giraffes, a small herd of blue wildebeests, a few red hartebeests and many impalas. The impalas would not let us get close enough to take a good shot at an aged male. As the sun grew hotter, we shed our extra layers of clothing. We crossed the main road cutting through the property and arrived back at the lodge around 10:30. I knew everyone was glad to be able to rest for a while out of the sun.

Rassie's daughter, Lana, had been cooking most of the meals and helping with laundry and other chores at the lodge. She was an excellent cook and prepared many great meals complete with exotic desserts. Rassie was very fortunate to have her help him with running the lodge during the day.

It wasn't long before we sat down to a wonderful meal prepared by Lana. Afterwards, we all gathered to the front of the lodge to take a group photo with the two trucks in the background.

I collected everyone's email address, so I could send them a copy of my journal after I got it typed on my computer. I hoped Jim would take my written story and some of the photos and make it into a finished book that everyone could have to remember our African adventure.

After lunch we started hunting again, and Doug finally had success in shooting a nice male impala. It was what he had been trying to accomplish for the past few days. The animal had been sitting on the ground when he first spotted it. He had his rifle mounted on the tripod sticks and aimed, as the impala got up. After being shot, it ran for seventy-five yards through the thick bush before falling. Doug located it within five minutes, as he followed the blood trail. The animal was loaded on the truck and we continued hunting.

Jim was the next to find an animal he was after. It was a vervet monkey, and he spotted one standing, facing away from us as we passed. Verwey steadied the tripod sighting sticks, and Jim shot the monkey, hoping it would not be too torn up for the taxidermist.

Jim later convinced Matt to hunt for a male impala, because he already had the beautiful zebra in the freezer. Twice Matt left the vehicle with Verwey, only to return with no success. I was told the impalas they were chasing had moved away from them as they approached. Afterwards, I sat in the truck on their last attempt of the day and heard a gunshot in the distance. I found out from Verwey that Matt had actually shot one. All we had to do was find it. According to Verwey, when he fired the shot from eighty yards and hit it in the chest, the animal almost fell forward. It then regained its balance and ran to the left through the bushes. It wasn't long before the five of us were searching for the impala that had left almost no blood trail.

By that time it was approximately 5:15, and the sun was quickly going down. We decided the thing to do would be to come back in the morning and resume the search. I hoped we could find that injured or dead animal, and that Matt could get it mounted. I knew it would be an excellent trophy and another lasting memory of his trip to South Africa, along with his zebra. I believed the male impala would have at least 22″ horns. We would see how it all turned out the next morning, when we began our last day of hunting.

We were up early on Friday. After a light breakfast, we quickly set out to search for Matt's wounded impala that had run away the previous evening. We arrived at the spot fifteen minutes later. Everyone fanned out and began to search in a line spanning 150 yards wide. As we walked, dodging the many six foot tall bushes and thorn trees located everywhere, the group gave maximum effort to finding the animal that could have been lying anywhere. We walked for 500 yards. Then we turned to cover another sector of that very large area.

After devoting an hour and a half to that effort, Verwey decided it was time to give up. We went back to his truck. It was time to drive back to the lodge, so we could meet with Cliff, the owner of the wildlife taxidermist business in Johannesburg. He was scheduled to come over and discuss how all the trophy animals would be mounted.

As we arrived at the lodge and entered the building, a fully cooked lunch was waiting to be consumed. We met Cliff, who was waiting for us. He turned out to be a nice, motivated businessman and was instantly liked. It was decided we would visit his wildlife mounting studio on Saturday on our way to the airport. We would decide with him how each animal would be positioned for mounting, based on seeing examples he had on display at his business.

After that meeting and lunch, both trucks left for an afternoon hunt that would be our last for the trip. Matt still hoped to bring down a trophy impala, and Jim wanted another kudu with horns in excess of 50″ in length. In the other truck, Bob Bible had decided to shoot a large blue wildebeest, which he finally accomplished early in the afternoon. As the story was told, his shot was perfect, and the blue wildebeest fell immediately when the bullet struck the animal. That had all been accomplished before Rassie could finish his instructions on exactly how to make the kill.

Matt and Verwey continued their efforts to find and kill a big male impala throughout the afternoon. Many times they started out through the vegetation to move in for a shot, but they were never able to get close enough before the animal ran away.

After we heard a rifle shot in the distance, Verwey received a cell phone call that Gary had shot and killed a big kudu. We were asked to drive to the area to help get the large animal to the truck and out of the dense brush. Upon arriving, we saw everyone standing around the kudu. Gary said the animal had fallen in its tracks with one shot. By looking at the animal, I guessed the horns to be 47" long, but they actually measured 50 ½". We found that the "greater kudus," of the extreme northern part of South Africa, truly had massive, spiraling horns and were larger than those living south of Johannesburg.

We went back to hunting with Verwey for the final hour of the evening and continued to look for a male impala until the sun went down. I told Verwey I really appreciated all his efforts and focus on trying to get Matt a trophy impala, but especially Verwey's successful efforts in helping Matt bring down the zebra two days earlier. Verwey was a super nice guy. I enjoyed being with him during the trip. We thanked Rassie, Verwey and Lana on being the perfect hosts. We let them know we looked forward to returning again in the future.

Everyone packed and loaded their gear on Saturday morning, and we left the lodge by 6:00. On our way to the airport, we stopped both vehicles at the wildlife mounting studio. After two hours, everyone had met individually with Cliff and worked out how they wanted their animals mounted. From his workshop, we purchased souvenirs of warthog tusks, small horns and animal skins to take with us.

After we arrived at the airport and checked our luggage, everyone shopped for curios in the small shops. We ate supper and boarded the plane. At 8:45 we lifted off for our 15 hour and 45 minute flight back to Atlanta. From there, after a five hour layover, I flew back to Wilmington completing my trip, while everyone else drove back to Nashville.

Overall, it had been my best trip to South Africa. Everyone seemed happy and satisfied with the whole experience. I had totally enjoyed spending the time with Matt, and knew he viewed it as a special opportunity to be with me.

*"Only those who attempt the absurd
can achieve the impossible."*

Albert Einstein

Australia
October 2016

In 2016, the World Masters Track and Field Championships were held in Perth, Australia. I signed up for the competition with great hopes of winning a medal. I knew the trip would also give Trent and me a chance to visit the country, which we might not have done otherwise. Trent set up an itinerary where we would first fly to Sydney. By stopping there, we could get our biological time clocks adjusted before flying across the continent to Perth. Our plans included visiting several additional areas around that country when the competition was over.

Excitement was in the air as we left home for our trip to Australia. We went to the Wilmington airport on October 20th with all our bags, plus my javelin. At the time, I really had no idea of the length of travel time necessary to get us all the way to Australia. We had to change planes in Charlotte, and then again in L.A., before we flew on to Sydney.

I was happy the planes were large enough to accept my javelin, so I didn't have to ship it by FedEx. I didn't want it held up in customs, as it had been for a previous meet in Nova Scotia, Canada. On that trip, my javelin barely made it to the stadium in time for the competition.

Our flight from L.A. to Sydney took close to fifteen hours. Traveling west across the Pacific Ocean, we went through many time zones and lost one full day on the calendar. On our return trip home four weeks later, I knew we would make up that lost day by flying east.

I was able to sleep five hours on the plane, but I had to watch four movies to fill the time. I'd always had trouble sleeping on a plane.

We landed in Sydney, Australia at 8:30 in the morning. The overall trip had taken thirty-one hours. Trent and I were both exhausted as we left our spacious "pod" seating in first class. Walking off the plane, I noticed there had been a light rain and the temperature was in the upper 60s. The forecast was for a pleasant day in the upper 70s. It was obvious to me, even though it was still early morning in Australia, we would need to get some additional sleep as soon as possible.

After picking up our luggage, we took a taxi to downtown Sydney. Everyone was very friendly when we were dropped off at the Sydney Harbor Marriott Hotel. Fortunately, our room was ready. We were taken to a nice room on the twenty-fifth floor overlooking the harbor. Out our window we could see a number of green and yellow ferryboats transporting people from the docks along the waterway.

I immediately recognized the world famous Sydney Opera House with its highly unusual roof. The roofline looked like multiple, billowing white sails placed side by side. The pattern created by that unique architecture had developed into an icon for Sydney, and Australia as a whole. As in all of the photos I had seen of that building, it was a beautiful structure. Trent took a photo using her Iphone and later sent it to our friends.

After eating a snack and watching a little television, we quickly fell asleep. When we woke five hours later, we went downstairs to explore the streets close to our hotel. Sydney had some very tall office buildings, and during our short walk on the first evening, I thought it looked like New York City.

We returned to the Marriott Hotel and went to the Executive Lounge to eat a meal "fit for a king." The food was delicious, and we found the extensive menu changed daily. As elite Marriott members, there was no charge. Because of that, we ended up eating most of our meals there.

Trent bought tickets for the next day so we could board an open bus and travel around the city. Our first stop the next morning was the Australian Museum of Science. I wanted to check out their display of dinosaur fossils. I knew Australia had once been connected to a much larger land mass called Pangea, but through tectonic activity of the surface areas, it had become an isolated island millions of years ago. The isolation had led to an evolution of animals and plants unlike any other on the earth. That diversification was documented by clever displays and exhibits throughout the museum. It was a fun trip that I really enjoyed.

We later walked through Hyde Park to see the early spring flowers of Australia. A stop at Hungry Jacks, otherwise known as Burger King, was a treat and something familiar. We stopped in a few roadside shops, and I bought an Australian flag. I had been trying to accumulate flags from the various countries we visited where I competed. So far, I had a nice collection back home.

The next day, we scheduled a tour to see the Sydney Opera House. When we walked from the hotel onto the pier near where it stood, I began to realize how large and spectacular it was. Its two-tone white and cream tiles on the top roof gleamed in the bright sunshine. Since the sky was solid blue with no clouds, the contrast of color made the building's architectural design really stand out.

As our guide took us through the inside of the building, he told us the roof design had gone through nineteen changes before the final design had been approved. Supposedly, the original architect who designed the structure never saw the finished project due to a disagreement with the builder. Inside, there were six large rooms where different types of performances were held throughout the year. The two largest rooms seated between 1,500 and 2,500 people. We had hoped to see *My Fair Lady* one evening while we were there, but the tickets were sold out.

In the afternoon, we stopped by an opal, mineral and fossil shop. The Australian opal is one of the most beautiful in the world with its strong blues, greens, reds, pinks and whites that shine with reflective iridescence. I asked the saleslady to show me some of the more valuable pieces of jewelry containing opals. She went into the back and returned with trays filled with stones set in gold and silver with diamonds. The first piece I asked about was priced at $250,000. I could hardly believe it. Others were priced at $150,000 and $75,000, and all were a surprise. There was one raw rock with a glazing of brilliant opal attached to the outer surface on one side only. That rock had obviously come directly out of the ground and was about eight inches long. It was priced at $50,000. It was amazing and very beautiful, but again, I could hardly believe the price.

The next day, we took a ten hour trip to the famous Blue Mountains west of Sydney. Alex, our driver, picked us up at the Marriott at 8:00. Off we went in his van, with eight other passengers, for a two hour drive. We first stopped at a spectacular "look-off ledge" that dropped abruptly 1,500 feet to a totally treed, green valley below. Just to look over the vertical ledge into the valley below was breathtaking.

From that spot, we drove to another location where we rode a sky lift from one mountain top to another inside a glass-enclosed cable car with a glass floor. On the other side of the mountain, we could see vertical rock cliffs that dropped clear to the valley floor. There were paths laid out, so we could walk down to the semi-tropical forest floor and see the lushness all around us. It was nature at its best.

To get back to the top, and to where our car was parked, we rode a train that ran almost vertically up the face of the mountain. The interesting thing about the ride up was that everyone faced backwards and looked downward, as we climbed to the top. It was like a roller coaster ride in reverse and in slow motion.

The Blue Mountains that swept the horizon contained a mist or light fog. Its trees were mostly a type of eucalyptus that was filled with oil, which supposedly evaporated into the air of the whole valley. From a distance, the sky had a light blue cast, and therefore the name.

As we left the mountains and began our trip back to Sydney, we stopped and ate lunch at a nice restaurant along the way. I ordered an Australian beer, named Cascade, with fried chicken, French fries and a salad. The white chicken meat had been pounded out flat and then pan fried. It was quite tasty and filled my stomach.

The final part of that day's long adventure was a three mile ferry ride. We boarded from a small pier and said good-bye to Alex, who had finished entertaining us with his stories about the area. The ferry ride carried us toward the city. We could see the tall buildings over the treetops. Again, it was a beautiful day with a bright blue, cloudless sky and calm water. We passed under the large, arched Sydney Harbor Steel Bridge, which framed our view of the Sydney Opera House. It gave us an opportunity to get a few photographs of that highly unusual structure from a different angle, as we passed right beside it on our way to the docking pier.

With the day's trip concluded, Trent and I walked a half of a mile through the city, past all kinds of shops, on our way back to the Marriott Hotel. A few hours later, and after some rest in the room, we rode the elevator downstairs for a nice supper. It had been a great day.

The next day, we were up early on our way to the domestic airport, so we could fly 2,000 miles west across the entire continent of Australia to arrive in Perth. That's where the World Masters Track and Field Championships were to take place over the next week. In that competition, I was planning to compete in the shot put and the javelin events in my five year, 65 to 69, age bracket.

When we arrived in Perth, I realized it was Halloween. A group of us, friends and track athletes from the U.S., had decided to rent two beach houses near the edge of the Indian Ocean.

Because those houses were in a neighborhood, we went to the store and bought candy in case we had some trick or treaters visit that evening. Later, a few kids did stop by. We had fun admiring their costumes while handing out the candy.

There were a total of twelve people staying in the two rented houses. In our house, we had Trent and me, Buzz, Betty, Clay, Shaaron and Joe. In the other house were Allen, Tammy, Mary, Steve and Anna. The whole group was very busy over the next few days sightseeing, shopping and participating in different competitive track events.

All of the track events were being held in two separate stadiums about 45 minutes apart. Both were a 50 minute drive from our houses. The first and more popular stadium was named the HBF stadium, an abbreviation for the Hospital Benefit Fund. I didn't understand the name, but the stadium was set up nicely for track and field activities with a large modern seating area overlooking the field.

On Saturday, I competed at the HBF stadium in the M65 shot put event, which included many good shot putters from around the world. It rained early in the day. That left the concrete thrower's ring wet when our competition started at 11:30. We were allowed only two warm up throws. That was really not enough and most of the athletes complained. In the actual competition, we were given six throws, with the first three throws determining who would advance to the top eight for the final round.

During my first three throws, I had one really good throw. As I stepped from the ring, I was feeling great. As I glanced back, I noticed the ring official holding up a red flag. That flag meant my throw had been ruled a foul and would not be counted. I could hardly believe what I had seen, so I went over to that official and asked what I had done to have the throw ruled a foul. He told me I had let the shot put drift slightly away from my neck, as I shifted into my final throwing position before starting my push upward. Never before had I experienced that ruling. I doubted what I was being told, so I had an intense discussion with him. The official would not change his decision. I walked away in disgust and hated that my best throw would not be counted.

After I threw three times, I realized the qualifying round had concluded. The officials looked over the results and picked out the top eight competitors for the final round. I was nervous because I knew I might not make it. When they announced the results, they read off my name as the person in eighth place. I had made the finals by a narrow margin and would be allowed three additional throws.

During the final three throws, I had one reasonable toss of 12.77 meters. That moved me up from eighth to fifth place. I never bettered that distance. The number four competitor finished with 12.91 meters. After the competition was over, I measured my earlier toss that had not been counted. It was 13.25 meters. It would have easily let me finish in fourth place instead of fifth.

The number one finisher, and gold medal winner, was an athlete from Norway with a throw just over 14 meters. The number two finisher, and silver medal winner, was a competitor from Switzerland who was only a short distance behind the first place finisher. The number three finisher, and bronze medal winner, was a competitor who had a throw of 13.41 meters. As I looked over those numbers, I realized I should have been able to reach the third place distance for a bronze medal, but it didn't happen. My best legal throw of 12.77 meters was just over 42 feet, and still pretty good for a man 67 years old.

Sunday, on our day off from competition, we drove to a wild animal park to see many of the strange creatures that lived in Australia. They included poisonous snakes, kangaroos, wallabies, wombats, Tasmanian devils and all kinds of beautiful tropical birds. We spent a lot of time in the gift shop looking over the unusual items associated with those animals.

My javelin event was scheduled for Tuesday afternoon at 4:15. I knew there would be a lot of very good javelin throwers competing, so I was anticipating a tough competition.

As I warmed up for the event, I could tell I was physically tired. My body strength and energy levels were down. I was still sore from the shot put competition. In spite of the weakness in my legs and lower back, I figured I could still have an acceptable outcome.

The qualifying round was ruled not necessary by the officials, so we proceeded directly into the finals. For the finals, each competitor was to get six throws in an effort to make it to the top three places for medals. After my first three throws, I found myself in second place, but I wasn't happy with my distance. I figured I needed to throw farther in order to finish with a medal. So far, my best throw had been less than 42 meters. I knew that was not going to be good enough.

I struggled mentally trying to achieve more quickness down the runway and more arm speed with the throw. I was having problems. With only one toss left in the competition, I was in third place. Then, on his very last throw, one of my competitors from Finland whom I had beaten three years earlier in Brazil, got a very good throw and passed me by one foot. Afterwards, my last throw did not land farther than his, so I finished in a depressing fourth place. I knew I had not done my best. It was embarrassing. All of my friends from the U.S. had been watching and cheering me from the stands.

As I left the field, after posing for photographs with the entire group of javelin throwers, my mind began to search for an excuse for not finishing higher in order to have been awarded one of the coveted world medals. As I looked inward, it was only me who was to blame.

I thought back about the previous few weeks, and all I had put myself through physically and mentally trying to get things done, just before taking the long trip to Australia. I had pushed myself to the limit. I had thought at the time I could recover physically and be just fine, but I realized that extra activity had taken a toll on my body. I had not been able to work out with weights and prepare properly for the Australian competition.

Weeks earlier, I had traveled to Greensboro, NC and participated in the USA Masters Games in 97 degree heat, where I won
three gold medals in the shot put, discus and javelin. I had then
traveled all the way to Vancouver, British Columbia, Canada
and won three additional gold medals in a large international
championship over a six day time period. That event, named
the Americas Masters Games, included fifty-two countries with
teams full of talented athletes.

I had a great time there. During the opening ceremony, the
organizers re-lit the huge Olympic flame from the 2010 Winter
Olympics. It burned for us during the entire competition and was
very impressive. When it was first lit during the ceremony, on
the banks overlooking a beautiful lake in downtown Vancouver,
I felt chills running up and down my spine. It was exciting to
have been there representing the United States as part of "Team
USA," but again, it took a lot out of me physically in the process.

After that very tiring trip to Vancouver, we traveled to Las
Vegas, Nevada for three days of competition in the Nevada
Senior Games. While there, I competed in five different events
and won all five of them. That included the weight throw, shot
put, discus, softball and javelin throw. As soon as I completed
the javelin event, we drove to St. George, Utah, so I could register at the convention center for the shot put event scheduled to
start the very next morning at 8:30. That event in Utah, named
the Huntsman World Senior Games, was another very large track
meet.

After two days of competition in Utah, I had won two more
gold medals. Even though I had originally signed up for the discus throw in addition to the shot put and javelin, I decided not to
throw the discus on the third day, so we could drive back early to
Las Vegas. I had already won seven gold medals in seven events
in two states.

Trent and I arrived back in Wilmington just in time to be hit
by Hurricane Matthew. That was a strong storm, which was

originally a Category Four. By the time it hit Florida's coast and worked upward through Charleston, SC, the winds had lowered from 160 mph to 100 mph, and it had become a Category Two hurricane. The eye of the hurricane passed directly over Wilmington. It made a mess of our yard.

After the storm passed, I started cleaning up the debris. It took me a day and a half to put everything back in order. There were small limbs and leaves everywhere. We only lost one tree in the backyard during those high winds, but it was an old rotten tree that needed to go anyway. After all that work, I was again exhausted.

Within hours of Hurricane Matthew leaving our area, my son John, his wife Mary Beth, and my two grandchildren Owen and Isabella, arrived at our house from Tennessee. Because of the storm, they had delayed their long eleven hour drive east from Nashville. John had not been able to come to Wilmington over the last fifteen years due to his limited vacation schedule, his new marriage and the birth of his two children. Because of that, I was definitely glad to see them. My problem was that while they were visiting, I didn't get to work out at the gym. I knew I needed to do that in order to maintain my strength.

John and his family stayed five days with us, and we did all kinds of fun activities together. It was a great time for me to be able to play with my grandkids. We went to the beach three times, played putt-putt golf, rode go-carts, went to the Fort Fisher Aquarium, went out to eat a few times, went shopping at Toys-R-Us and went to the Eclipse Art Gallery, where I had three of my large bronze sculptures on display for sale.

During all that time, I knew I should have been going to the gym daily and working out. I couldn't force myself to pull away from my family, even for a few hours. I also knew I needed to go to the local university's track and prepare for the upcoming world competition by actively throwing the shot put and javelin. It just wasn't in the cards for me. I kept thinking

I would be able to overcome that lack of activity and still do well in Australia.

Within hours of John and his family leaving Wilmington, I had to rent a U-Haul trailer and drive to my bronze foundry in Atlanta, GA to try and finish a major piece of sculpture that was scheduled to be installed at a small park in Wilmington. That trip to Atlanta was 475 miles. I arrived there late Sunday evening after a long nine hour trip. Due to the hurricane, many of the roads were still covered with water. I was forced to drive out of my way to bypass the flooding.

On Monday morning, I waited outside the foundry in Atlanta until 8:00 ready to get started helping the metal chasers finish my piece. They assured me it would be completed by noon the next day. As the day progressed, I could see we were having a time problem. There was more to be done than I had expected.

I agreed late Monday evening to be at the foundry by 5:00 the next morning to get an early start. I was up at 3:00 and anxious to get going, so the project could be finished. By 10:00, the piece was ready to sandblast, but it still would need the patina added. I knew that process was time consuming work. The owner told me that one of his workers could add the patina, seal it, have it totally dry and loaded in my trailer by noon. I should have known that was not possible, because I have never had a large bronze sculpture's patina added in less than five hours.

On top of everything, the main guy who normally added the patina didn't show up for work that day. Another employee assured me he could handle the job in record time. As I stood around and watched the patina of special acids being added with an industrial blowtorch, I could tell it was not going well. The employee doing the work was not doing an acceptable job.

Finally, at 1:00, I decided to call a halt to what was happening. I knew then I had wasted my valuable time and money trying to get the work done, just before leaving for Australia and my big competition. I simply told the owner I had to leave. I could not wait any longer for the finished sculpture. I knew I still had a nine hour drive back to Wilmington.

When I arrived back in Wilmington very early Wednesday morning, I knew I had to go right to bed and get some sleep. Later that day, I would have to get organized, packed, and be off to the airport for the start of our trip to Australia. I was completely exhausted.

All of what I just described happened within a few weeks before leaving for Australia. I included the details, as part of the story, to point out I had done way too much physically prior to going and wasn't prepared for the big competition. I had just hoped I would be able to do well in the shot put and javelin when the time came. As it turned out, I didn't have my normal competitive edge that was required. I did well, but I didn't win one of the three medals. That was what I had really wanted to achieve.

When the track competition was over in Perth, Trent and I flew to Adelaide on the south edge of Australia where we spent a few days relaxing. We stayed downtown at the Hotel Grand Chancellor. From there, we made a few side trips to see the area, but mostly just hung out. The other athletes disbursed in all directions. Some headed home and others set out to visit different parts of the country.

From Adelaide, we went south to Kangaroo Island. We had to travel on a ferry across the open ocean. The aqua colored water looked smooth and calm, but as we approached the ferry, I realized the water was quite choppy. I began to worry because I easily get sea sick.

As soon as we pulled away from the dock, my stomach began to churn with the constant sway of the boat. There were four single chairs in front of my long seat. All four began to swing 360 degrees round and round on swivels. Trent told me to move to the back of the boat, but I was already too sick to move. Luckily, there was no one else sitting on my bench. I lay down and faced backward with my chest pressed against the back of the seat.

That trip across the choppy water lasted forty-five minutes, and I could hardly wait to get to shore. In my world, it was the "trip from hell." After the water crossing, we boarded a medium sized van driven by a man named Conway, and started another one hour thrill ride. He drove eighty miles an hour. I expected a grown male, 160 pound kangaroo to hop out of the undergrowth into the road at any time and cause a terrible accident. We had been warned by others it could happen, so I was quite nervous during the entire ride.

We arrived at the Ozone Hotel none too soon, as it was beginning to get dark. After a nice meal in the hotel's restaurant, we went to bed, still alive.

The next day we started an island tour with the Odessey Tour Company. A pleasant guide named Mark Kelly was in charge. He drove much more reasonably and told us all about the island and its wildlife as we traveled along. We were with him for two days, as he took us to all the interesting sites. We got to see mobs of kangaroos. Some contained as many as 75 individuals. We saw two types of seals on the north and south sides of the island.

We learned Kangaroo Island was approximately 95 miles long and 50 miles wide. It was known for its many unusual animals, birds, snakes and flowering plants. The red bottlebrush plant, the Cape daisy (that was bright yellow and filled in the open fields), and the large bunches of blue flag iris were all native plants to admire. There were many varieties of eucalyptus trees in the fields and along the roadsides. We saw a venomous black snake crawling across the road and a few dark brown and yellow striped lizards two and a half feet long.

On the second day, we visited an iconic site on the southwest overlooking the ocean from a hilltop, where there were huge house-size granite boulders clustered all alone by themselves. The boulders were very unusual and stood out from all the other rolling hills. They had been named the Remarkable

Rocks. They looked like a small fort on top of the rise. There was orange-colored plant lichen growing on the rocks' surface. It gave those particular boulders a color not seen anywhere else in the area.

We also visited a bay with a wooden walkway that lead down a hill. There were two dramatic, uninhabited stone islands just off shore. The waves crashed against them so violently that occasionally large sprays would jump one hundred feet into the air. As we walked farther down the wooden walkway, we came to a huge, open, natural stone arch. It was absolutely immense and named the Admiral's Arch. From out of the dark opening where we were standing, I could see bright sunshine hitting the rocks near the ocean and the crashing surf below. There were fur seals sitting on the rocks or venturing out to sea trying to find something to eat. We were told they had to avoid the great white sharks that constantly roamed the area looking for an easy seal meal. With all the seals and the great white sharks, it would not have been a place to either swim or surf.

Another place of interest led us to a spot where we found a group of small, kangaroo type animals, called wallabies. We also saw cockatoos and various green and multi-colored parakeets.

Our guide took us on a journey to find koalas in their natural habitat. We stopped in an open field, lined by large eucalyptus trees, and began our search. All I had to do was look through the trees about halfway up. Right away, I spotted one twenty feet off the ground. The koala sat quietly in the fork of small limbs, giving the impression it might fall to the ground as it slept. It looked like the toy teddy bear we all played with as kids. There were two rounded ears facing forward that were quite fuzzy. The bear had small brown eyes buried in light gray, soft brown and white hair, and a dark nose, making it look very sweet and cute.

After staring at that first sighting, our small group proceeded through the growth of trees and spotted a total of twenty of those cuddly koala bears. Some were wedged in the tree limbs as low as ten feet above our heads. They made no noise and just stared down at us with sleepy eyes. There were two koalas holding babies. The babies were exact duplicates of the adults but much smaller and maybe ten inches tall. The adults were probably two feet tall and weighed approximately thirty-five pounds. Their whole diet consisted of eating slender leaves off the eucalyptus trees. We were told that was where they got their water supply.

The next day we traveled back to the main shore. We again stayed in Adelaide for one night before flying to the northeast section of the continent, to a city named Cairns, pronounced "Canns." That city was on the coast across from the world famous Great Barrier Reef. We planned to stay at the Alamanda Palm Cove Hotel, located ten miles west of Cairns, for the next five days.

Once there, I looked out of our glass balcony door toward the ocean from the third floor. I couldn't help but notice the bright sun filtering through a line of palm trees between us and the beach. The light breeze was gently moving the palm fronds creating a very relaxing mood. The temperature must have been around eighty degrees with beautiful blue skies. I felt like I was in paradise.

The next morning, we signed up for a nine hour bus tour that would leave the Palm Cove Hotel within the hour. The destination was Daintree National Park, 50 miles west of where we were staying. The first 23 miles were along the coast on a winding road full of hairpin turns. Both Trent and I nearly got sick. After finally stopping, we discussed canceling the remainder of the trip and renting a private car to take us back to the hotel. We decided to stick it out so we could see the rainforest. By the end of the day, we were glad we had not gone back early.

First, we stopped along the roadside to see a tea packaging company. There was machinery which harvested the three foot high green plants that grew in rows forming very thick bushes. The leaves, after being harvested and dried, were then ground, baked and packaged for sale.

In the rainforest, we saw about fifteen mint stick insects that were supposedly very rare. The guide told us the three inch long blue and green insects only existed in that one little area and lived on the leaves of a special plant. If touched, it would spray a poisonous mist on the victim. If a human were sprayed, he would suffer bad diarrhea as a result. There were supposed to only be around three hundred of them left in the world. If that was right, and I doubted the claim, we saw a large percentage of the remaining ones.

We stopped at different overlooks along the way to view the ocean that revealed islands out in the distance. We also stopped to walk down to a few long, isolated beaches. The paths where we walked were covered by large trees creating a canopy. As we went through those areas, the thick trees didn't allow much light to reach the forest floor.

We took an hour long boat ride down the muddy and narrow Daintree River in search of crocodiles. We only saw two small babies, eighteen inches long, and a larger one about seven feet long. There were supposed to be others in the river up to eighteen and twenty feet long, but we didn't see them.

During our ride back to the hotel, someone in the back of the van announced Donald Trump had just won the Presidential election. It was November 9th in Australia. That person had been searching for current news on his Iphone and found out the information. I was very excited and happy to hear the news, but I found most of the Australians on the van thought it was terrible he had won. For me, it again just pointed out how the liberal media, which favored only Hillary Clinton, had influenced the entire world with its one-sided reporting. I couldn't wait to get back to our room to watch the results on television. When I eventually was able to turn on our television, it was 2:00 a.m.

back home. Trump was in the process of making a speech, and Hillary had just called him on the phone to concede her loss.

After sleeping for only five hours, I was excited and got up very early in the morning to hear Hillary Clinton's live speech stating she was shocked she had lost. Just the day before the election, Hillary had been picked by all the liberal media polls to win with an 87% certainty.

That morning we drove to Port Douglas. There we boarded the Quick Silver tour boat to take us to the Great Barrier Reef. We drove our own rental car, so both of us had much less trouble with the winding roads. It was a sunny, calm day. The water was still and flat inside the reef. We traveled on a large catamaran boat for an hour and a half to get to a special spot near the reef where we could snorkel. The Quick Silver tour group owned a large, stationary platform, which held about four hundred people, and that was where we started our snorkeling adventure.

I was excited to get to snorkel the Great Barrier Reef, but was also wary of the small, highly venomous box jelly fish I knew were in the area. We had been told those creatures were in the waters near the beaches because of the light breezes blowing toward the shore. On our trip, we were a few miles out in the ocean near the inner edge of the reef. In spite of that, we were offered tight fitting, full body Lycra suits to protect us. I rented one of those suits with no hesitation.

With a furnished mask, snorkel and fins, I entered the crystal clear water. Trent was right behind me. Stepping down off the metal platform that allowed easy access to the ocean, we could immediately see large fish swimming around us in all directions.

There was one fish, with a natural hump on its head that was obviously a pet. I had to step over it on the last, large step which was two feet under water. The body of the fish was covered with beautiful colors of blue, green, brown, gray and rust. It was about three feet in length. The colors varied and included spots, lines and blotches. Beside the platform, I also noticed a very large, slow moving fish that looked like a brown grouper. When I asked the helpers standing on the metal steps, they told me it was a Queensland grouper weighing around two hundred pounds.

Trent and I pushed off the steps and snorkeled toward the open reef with high expectations. The water below was forty to fifty feet deep, but it quickly became shallow, as we reached the edge of the reef. There were all types, shapes and colors of living coral below us. I recognized fields of staghorn coral with its long, zagged edges in colors of white, cream and blue. I saw plate coral, brain coral and other types of coral I had not seen before.

As we moved over the reef, smaller, colorful fish began to appear. I had to only float along to observe the wonder below. I saw a few yellow, black and white fox face fish eight inches long. They were fat and healthy. Up until that time, I had only seen those in books or in saltwater marine aquariums.

There were different species of parrotfish in shades of pastel pink, violet, green, yellow, rust and deep blue. I noticed a mated pair of ornate butterfly fish seven inches long with rounded silver colored bodies and stripes of orange, yellow and black. The only other time I had seen those was while snorkeling in the shallow waters of Hawaii.

Ten feet away, I saw a saddleback butterfly fish moving toward me with it characteristic black patch angling over the top rear of its body. It was ten inches long, and as it passed me I noticed other distinct details on its face. I had become familiar with that fish while carving and painting a sculpture of one five years earlier. I had also carved and painted two of the ornate butterfly fish. It was good to be able to observe them up close and in the wild.

At the edge of the reef, I noticed a familiar shape. As I moved closer, I confirmed it was indeed what I had thought, a giant clam. It was open and feeding with a zagged shell mouth extending close to four feet in length. The inner skin included white moving tissue, and there was a three inch tube extending from one end that pulled water in and out of the clam.

We saw other types of fish as they swam by us. As I moved over the reef below, every nook and cranny seemed to hold a new wonder. I even saw a turtle swimming nearby. I moved closer, so I could get a better view of its body. It moved slowly, and I kept a short distance away from it so it would not be afraid.

We left the water after an hour of snorkeling. We didn't want to miss the buffet that had been prepared on the deck. There were all types of salads, pasta, fried chicken, prawns on ice, breads and potatoes. It was a very good meal.

Next, we proceeded to another area and took a ride on an underwater boat that had windows on both sides of the vessel. The water was very calm. We were comfortable moving through the reef watching the large coral and fish move by us through the glassed windows.

After that glass-sided boat trip, we walked down steps to a underwater stationary viewing area. We were completely dry, as we again looked through glass windows. That area was positioned at another spot on the large stationary platform where our ship had docked.

Shortly afterward, it was time to return to shore. We chose our seats and began the long trip back to Port Douglas. The large ship, carrying around four hundred of us, moved very fast and made good time.

The next day, Trent and I had the day off from scheduled tours. We decided to drive ten miles down the coast to the town of Cairns to do some souvenir shopping. When we parked our rental car in the basement of a large hotel, we noticed a casino entrance near the door of the garage. I figured Trent wanted to check it out, so I suggested we go inside and gamble for a short time.

Immediately, we noticed an active roulette table and started betting $2.50 chips. After half an hour of going up and down, we left the table losing about $30. Trent then found an unusual slot machine and began to push the buttons while I stood and watched. She was quickly down about $20 and then hit a small jackpot of $55. She collected her winnings, and we cashed out. Our short gambling experience had left us $6 ahead. I kept a $5 chip from the roulette table for a nice souvenir.

For the next couple of hours, we wandered through various shops and bought a few small items. After making a brief stop at Hungry Jacks, we decided to stop at an opal mine exhibit. We had seen an outside billboard advertisement that a video could be seen about the mining of that rare mineral at the exhibit. We again were reminded, from watching the video, that Australia had some of the most beautiful opals in the world.

The next morning, on Saturday, we decided to go on another organized tour that included a long tram ride up and down a nearby mountainside. It ended with a train ride at the end of the day. Our outing lasted from 8:30 in the morning until 5:00 in the afternoon. Most of that time was spent on the Kuranda Skyrail and the Kuranda Scenic Train.

We boarded the skyrail, which had glass windows and a special glass floor for viewing downward. It lifted us up the steep mountain and over the tropical rain forest. The skyrail was enclosed, but otherwise it was similar to riding a regular ski lift. As we rose upward, I could see clear across the town of Cairns, all the way to the ocean. The panoramic view of the buildings below and in the distance, the open ocean, and the islands were incredible. I was able to look straight down through the glass bottom to see orchids growing on the rainforest trees, along with many ferns and interesting plants. Everything was very green. In most places the forest floor was not visible.

The skyrail trip included a short walk through the rainforest and then a second stop to view a huge 285 meter waterfall. The water moving over the waterfall ran through the Barron Gorge with very steep, treed hillsides. We were shown pictures of the waterfall during the rainy season. It looked like Niagara Falls in miniature with all of its water and mist.

Once we arrived at the end of our skyrail trip, we unloaded at a small town that included many shops full of unusual souvenirs. After a quick lunch, we went shopping. I bought narrow, center sections of two crocodile hides that were five feet long and six inches wide. I figured that my younger son, Matt, could make a neat guitar strap out of one of them. I planned to hang the other one on my wall at home. We purchased some interesting place mats and a beautiful hand painted bowl to be used either for display or for serving hors oeuvres.

After shopping, we boarded the Kuranda Scenic Train that was built in 1913. It included twenty passenger cars with two large electric engines that pulled us through fifteen tunnels and over more than fifty bridges. The inside of the train was beautiful and ornate. It reminded me of what the Orient Express probably looked like in past years. The train ride lasted for an hour. We were served drinks and food including cheeses and frozen mango ice cream. The weather was hot all day, hovering around 92 degrees, so light breezes were welcomed as we moved along.

The next day, we flew to Sydney in preparation for leaving Australia. That morning we decided to go to an authentic aborigine show that included dancing and singing by a large number of locals. One of them played an instrument original to the natives called a "didgeridoo." They wore body paint all over their bodies and put on quite a show.

Afterwards, they took us outside and showed us how to throw a boomerang and an Australian spear. I found that very interesting and participated with great interest. The spear throwing was very similar to the throwing of a javelin. It took a short while to get used to both items, especially the spear, because they used an additional device that hooked into the tail end of the spear to add leverage to the throw. Those spears were used to hunt animals for food. They were very serious when giving the instructions.

After the show was over, Trent and I just hung around because we had two hours to kill before we had to be at the airport. I went over and sat down to talk to three of the aborigines who were painting on small stones they later sold to tourists. They spoke good English, so we had a nice conversation. They were very interested in knowing about the United States and asked me many questions. All three of them indicated they would like to sometime travel to our country.

I asked them about Australia and their native culture. They openly talked about their customs and the way they had been raised. As I observed them while we talked, I noticed how different their features were from Americans. If I were to try and describe what I'm talking about, I would say they had body features similar to the now extinct Neanderthals. They were short and stocky with very squared off foreheads. Their skin was dark, and they had very coarse hair on their bodies.

I enjoyed spending the time with them. As I left, they asked me to take one of their painted rocks to remember them by. I was very glad to get it and thanked them. I gave them some money for the painted stone, even though they didn't ask for any. I now have it placed on my desk by my computer and use it as a paper weight to remind me of the trip.

It was interesting how much of a positive impression I gained about Australia from just the short two hours I spent with the three natives, while waiting for our flight out of Sydney. The entire trip was enjoyable, and we had a great time. Maybe sometime in the future, we can go back.

*"Write in your heart
that every day
is the best day of the year."*

Ralph Waldo Emerson

South Korea
March 2017

At noon on Thursday, March 16th, I was at the Wilmington International Airport waiting to board my plane to Charlotte. The start of my long journey to Daegu, South Korea for the 2017 World Masters Track and Field Indoor Championships was about to begin.

My plans were to document this trip through my writings so I could later relive the memories and adventures.

From Wilmington, my first plane flew to Charlotte, and then I took another one to Dallas, Texas. In Dallas, I spent the night and the next morning took an American Airlines flight straight into Seoul, South Korea. South Korea is located between the mainland of China and Japan, about halfway around the globe.

In Dallas, there were five track athletes from around the United States who were waiting to take the same plane to Seoul. One man wore an Atlanta Track Club Elite Team shirt. I told him I was also a member of that special team. A small group of us on that team were sponsored by the Muzuno Athletic Apparel Company. We had a nice visit, and I wished him well in the competition.

I stayed inside the airport in Seoul during my four hour layover because of political unrest, protests, and a few killings that had recently occurred in that city. I then boarded a Korean Airlines flight for the final part of the trip that took me to Daegu, South Korea. Daegu was where the competition would take place. My schedule was to throw the javelin on Monday and the shot put on Tuesday. On Wednesday, March 22, I would reverse the route to get home, except for a three hour train trip from Daegu back to Seoul. It was rumored the pilots of Korean Airlines would be going on strike starting March 22nd.

Most of the other U. S. athletes had planned to take the train going both ways between Seoul and Daegu because it was cheaper than flying. The three hour train ride cost $58.00.

I was hoping a few Koreans would be able to understand my "southern English." Otherwise, my communication would be by crude sign language, as I had done in 2005 while in Argentina where everyone spoke Spanish.

I didn't plan to wear anything displaying the USA logo during my travels until getting into the main stadium where special uniforms were required for competition. That was the advice we had received from officials before leaving home. I knew it would help avoid problems. I planned to travel, as much as possible, with the other athletes. We had been given some very nice, team uniforms by USATF to wear, and I was anxious to put mine on. About 100 individuals from the United States, both male and female, were to compete in the world championship. Many of them were friends.

My expert "travel agent," Trent, had planned everything for me before I left home. We went over the itinerary the morning before she dropped me off at the airport. It was like I was a little kid who had his mother pack his lunch in a brown paper bag and was about to board the school bus on his way to the first grade on his first day of school. That kid didn't know exactly what to expect, but he was excited and ready to take on a new experience.

In Daegu, I picked up my luggage and javelin around 9:00 p.m. While leaving the airport to catch a taxi, there was a lady with a sign for the shuttle going to the InterBurgo Hotel. I asked her if it was for the InterBurgo Hotel-Daegu where I had a reservation, and she said, "Yes."

In the back of my mind it seemed too easy, but I gladly loaded all my belongings on the shuttle bus. The driver could not speak English. After twenty minutes, I was dropped off at the hotel. At the front desk, I found out it was the wrong one. It was the InterBurgo Hotel-Expo. The desk clerk told me to take a twenty to thirty minute taxi ride across town, so that was my next move. That driver also spoke no English. Traveling through the middle of downtown Daegu, there were no signs I could read. I paid by credit card, trusting the driver to charge me correctly, which worked out to be $10.

I was let off at the InterBurgo Hotel-Daegu at 10:00. While exiting the taxi, I breathed a sigh of relief. It had been a long day, starting in Dallas, when I had first arrived at the airport in the early morning. That seemed like a week ago.

My room on the fifth floor had no air conditioner. The bell-man, who had helped me with my luggage, opened a window which would only move about one foot to let in the night air. After he left, I saw something strange under a table and picked it up. It was an emergency, in case of fire, box containing a sturdy rope only 35 feet long, a flashlight, and an unusual smoke mask. Looking out of the window, it was obvious if one end of that rope was tied around something stable in the room, I would do well to get down the wall to the fourth floor, much less all the way to the ground.

I turned on the television and found there were hundreds of stations, but they all seemed to be broadcast in Korean. My routine of watching television to pass the time would obviously not work out. Oh well, the good thing was I had successfully made it to Daegu!

On Sunday morning, a shuttle took me to the main stadium where I registered and picked up my bib number, "65065," at the TIC center. Then I walked to Stadium C, three-quarters of a mile away, to check-in my javelin and see the field layout where everyone would be throwing the next morning. After a few efforts of going in the wrong direction because all the signage was written in Korean, the area was located and my javelin was given to the officials. It was weighed and measured, and also checked to make sure it had the legally allowed center of balance. It was approved and then impounded in a storage bin, where I was told to pick it up right before starting the competition the following morning.

Because I was free on Sunday afternoon, the tour desk was checked to see what tours might be available from one o'clock to six o'clock. There was only one. It cost $90 and was going to three places. Those included the ancient capital city of Gueongju at Cheomseongdae, a large park with a huge man-made lake at the Bomun Tourist Complex, and a separate visit to the Bulguksa Temple where people went to pray to a large, gold-gilded Buddha statue. I took that tour knowing it might be the only time I had to see the sights.

The first stop was to the ancient capital city before it had been moved to Daegu. The city had served as the capital for approximately 1,000 years and still contained many huge dirt mounds containing ancient burials near the main road. Surrounding them was a public park full of kids flying kites with their parents. I was told by the tour guide that the city once numbered one million residents, but now only 300,000 people lived there.

In contrast, the main city of Daegu contained two and a half million people, while the entire country of Korea had fifty-one million. Many of the people in Daegu lived in very tall, high rise apartments scattered around in clusters. I noticed on the trip how clean the air seemed in comparison to cities I had visited a few years earlier in neighboring China. The main difference was that China's major cities were full of factories burning coal to create energy, and the resulting pollution with its gray smog filled the air everywhere.

The second stop on our tour was to a large lake, surrounded by hotels, with many cherry trees about to burst into bloom. We moved along fairly quickly in that area and were told we were in the early days of spring on March 19th. That surprised me because even though I had traveled so far around the world, the season was about the same as North Carolina's.

Our third stop was to an ancient wooden and highly decorated temple complex built originally in 751 A.D. that contained many buildings. All of them were very old, but they were still ornate in spite of having been burned to their stone foundations a few hundred years earlier by an invading country. That rebuilt temple complex reminded me very much of the Forbidden City I had visited a few years earlier in China. The one in Korea was different because it was still actively being used to worship Buddha. As we walked from building to building, we watched people go into the area to kneel and pray.

We arrived back at the main stadium just in time to get involved in the opening ceremony. Approximately one hundred Team USA athletes marched together around the track in the stadium in matching uniforms. In front and behind us were other teams from more than 100 different countries. The varying colors of the uniforms, and the happy, smiling athletes in the celebration, were something special to see. Each time I've been a part of that type of ceremony, I have gotten cold chills running up and down my body because it reminded me of the Summer Olympics and their opening ceremony celebration. In various world competitions, I've now participated many times, and it has always been a thrill.

After eating a good buffet dinner served at the hotel, I retired to my room to get some rest. The next morning I would be off to the stadium with high hopes of a good finish in the javelin competition. That night, I dreamed about the upcoming event and visualized myself being on the top level of the award podium for the medal ceremony.

Monday started at 5:00 a.m. I had slept for only six hours because of being too excited to go back to sleep once awake. After cleaning up, I read a book to occupy the next two hours in order to stay relaxed. At 7:00 a.m., the breakfast buffet started. I went down and enjoyed only a "lite" meal, so as to not be too full when the competition started in less than three hours. Afterwards, I went back to my room and quickly changed into my uniform. Just before going to sleep the previous night, I had laid out all my clothes and the other items needed.

In front of the hotel, I found the correct shuttle bus that would take me to the main stadium. There were other shuttles also taking athletes to various locations around the large athletic complex, so I didn't want to get on the wrong one. Outside, the morning was overcast, gloomy and very cold. Gray clouds and heavy fog covered everything. I could only see a hundred yards in the distance.

In retrospect, with more thought, I would have waited another hour before leaving the hotel, because I ended up outside in the open stadium with the freezing cold air. My body was chilled, even though I was bundled up in a variety of layered clothing. The javelin throwing field at stadium C was out in the open, and all of the rooms under the large seating areas were locked. There were two portable heaters, but they were out of fuel. I tried to keep moving and jogged a few times around the track to stay warm and loose while waiting.

The time passed quickly and all the competitors soon reported to the call room, which had to be done forty minutes before we started the actual competition. Our javelins had been weighed earlier, checked for legal balance, and measured before being held overnight. They were taken directly to the javelin runway at the same time the officials marched us to that area.

We were then allowed to begin our short practice session where each of us was allowed three practice throws. I had trouble loosening up because it was so cold. All of the other competitors from the different countries had the same problem. I noticed there were so many different languages being spoken that most of us were communicating by using simple sign language. It was almost comical.

I figured my biggest threats in the competition would come from the countries of Kazakhstan and Finland, based on the registration distances each individual had entered as his best throw during the past year. There were others with very good throws from Estonia, Australia, Czech Republic, Germany, Japan and Korea. A good throw would certainly be needed to be in the running for one of the three medals. My goal was to take home either a gold, silver or bronze medal.

We started with eight officials controlling the activity. They had us scheduled for only six throws each, including three for the qualifying round and then three for the final round. The winner would be the person who could throw the javelin the farthest in the air and get the point to hit the ground before any other part of the spear hit, while keeping it within the right and left sector lines on the field. The rules also required that every competitor keep his entire body behind a fixed, final throwing line. There were two officials watching that very closely. We could use the entire runway, a distance of 114 feet, to run and pick up speed before the final release. I used only 69 feet of that distance for my throws.

My first official throw in the qualifying round did not come out of my hand correctly and therefore drifted slightly sideways, creating some air resistance. It ended up being only an average throw, and I knew a better throw was necessary. During my three warm ups, one toss had been really good. If I could repeat that during the official competition, I was certain to win one of the three highly prized medals. That was all I was focused on while watching the other competitors complete their first throws.

When it was time in the rotation for me to take my second throw, I noticed on the rack of approved javelins one that was made in Europe. It had a seventy-five meter rating. Mine was a seventy meter javelin. If I could get it to come out of my hand correctly and stick in the ground point first, I was sure it would sail a long way.

The trick in throwing the seventy-five meter javelin was that you had to be able to throw it a long distance, with extra power, to get the point to come down first. That was critical. Otherwise, it would just hit the ground flat and be ruled a foul, which made it an illegal throw.

Because of not being required to use my own javelin, the seventy-five meter javelin was picked up with confidence. I stood silently at the start of the runway. An extra moment was taken to visualize it sailing high in the air and leveling off while powering forward for a winning distance.

An additional thought struck me that had been offered weeks earlier by a good friend, Ben Byrd, back in North Carolina. It involved an inner technique of calming my mind and relaxing my body with intense focus before a throw. Because of that, I bounced on my toes to relax and tried to steady and focus my busy mind.

It was time to make the throw. All that was in my head was the objective to move quickly and throw as hard as I could, while screaming on release to allow my muscles to explode with total body energy. Everything clicked perfectly, and I hit the final body position correctly. While releasing the javelin and gaining control of my follow-through, I stared upward toward the dot in the sky, which was my javelin racing away from me. I knew while it was in the air it would sail far, based on how it came off my fingertips. When it stuck in the ground, there was no doubt it was a good throw because it had landed on top of the very last marked line far in the distance.

The throw was quickly ruled legal by the field official. I had not stepped on or over the final throwing line at the end of the runway. As a result, those two officials held up white flags and the electronic measurement came back to the main record keeper. Not being able to understand Korean as he announced the measurement, I walked over to the recorder's table to check the written distance on his note pad. It was listed as 45 meters, and I was thrilled.

Slowly, I watched all the other competitors take their remaining qualifying throws that determined the top eight individuals who would go into the finals for an additional three throws. The top eight competitors were reassigned a new throwing order based on how they had done in the qualifying round. My name was in last place on the list, meaning I had the best throw in the qualifying round and would have the very last throw in the final round of the competition.

The last three throws of the finals began. I watched the other athletes, one at a time, give it their best. At any moment I could be beaten, and my breath was held nervously as each person released their spears into the air. All of their attempts fell just shy of that farthest marked line I had hit on my second throw.

Finally, while standing on the runway ready to make my last throw, the announcement was made that I had already won the competition. A chill ran down my back, and a smile appeared on my face. I had finally won a world championship. Twice in the past few years, I had placed second in the world, once in Brazil in 2013 and once in France in 2015. I had wanted to win a world competition in my five year age bracket, and now at almost 68 years of age, that had been accomplished. I was completely overjoyed.

My final throw was taken with all of that in mind, and the javelin traveled high in the air but landed just shy of where my second throw had landed. It was also a great throw, but my second throw was the one that won the competition.

While leaving the runway, all of the other competitors and officials began to clap. It was a response from them as to how much they respected my outcome. I went to each one individually to shake their hand. There were smiles everywhere as everyone congratulated me. I was riding high on adrenalin. It was then announced that a limo was to take the three top finishers from stadium C back to the main stadium for the medal presentation that was to happen within the hour.

I had finished first for the United States. The athlete from Estonia finished second, seven feet behind me, and the athlete from the Czech Republic came in third, only one foot behind him. One of the competitors from Finland, who had beaten me by only a few inches on his last throw in another world competition in Australia, finished in fourth place and out of the medals.

We were escorted to the waiting limo, with all our belongings, and taken directly to the three-tiered podium in the main stadium where the medals were to be presented. The flag of the United States was displayed behind the center and top level of the podium where I stood. After the gold medal was placed around my neck, the American National Anthem was played. Tears formed in my eyes from my pride. I continued to hold my right hand over my heart while looking at another American flag out in front of me. It was a special moment, and many people in the crowd took photos of the event.

While on the top tier of the awards podium, I invited the second and third place finishers, Lembit Talpsett and Vladimir Srb, to step up to that level with me so we could stand side by side to celebrate the moment for a combined photo showing our new world medals. When we stepped off the podium, the entire area broke into a standing ovation. It was awesome.

As I left the area, person after person approached and wanted a photo taken with me. I gladly agreed. They said to me they wanted a picture while standing with a "world champion." It made me feel like a celebrity. Later, I found out I was the first U. S. athlete to have won a gold medal on that first day of competition. What an honor. I was elated while walking through the crowd with my javelin in my hand and a gold medal around my neck. I was sure I would never forget the experience.

It rained all night Monday, and the next morning I noticed through the window of my room that everything was soaked and messy outside. In addition, it was still very cold. It was the day when my shot put competition was to take place at 12:00 noon. Fortunately, I was scheduled to throw inside stadium B with a roof over my head. That building was large and was set up on a hill similar to the main stadium.

I began to think about the previous day after finally getting back to my room from the javelin competition. After lying down on the bed at 4:00 p.m., I slept until 10:30 p.m. Because of that, I hadn't eaten any supper, but did get some badly needed rest. I had then fallen asleep again at midnight and had woken up at 4:00 a.m., while it was still dark outside. My body was sore all over, so I began to question my original plans to enter the shot put competition. Because there was an outside chance of winning a medal, I decided to go ahead and compete.

Around 10:00 a.m., I caught a shuttle bus to the main stadium, and then walked half a mile up a gentle hill to stadium B. All the competitors assembled in the call room at 11:30 so everyone could get checked in before we were all led to the inside shot put ring. We were allowed only three warmup throws and quickly we were under way. Two of my warmup throws were good. I was feeling energized as the event began.

My first official throw was average, but I knew there was a real chance to get one of the three medals. My second throw of 12.15 meters, over 40 feet, put me in second place. The competitor from Estonia got an early toss of 12.09 meters and that put him less than one inch behind me for third place. The early leader from Poland threw 12.51 meters. The throwing ring was extremely slick, and that was causing me trouble with getting traction and staying focused.

After the first three qualifying throws were completed, we were put in reverse order, with me next to last on the list. That meant I was in second place halfway through the competition with the final eight qualifiers getting three more throws. With each new throw by every other individual, I felt more and more anxious that at any time they might better my distance and move me down in the order.

As it turned out, my last four throws all slipped off the side of my hand. I was unable to better my second throw which had been a very average distance for me. I had been trying too hard and was not relaxed. My feet had not shifted correctly under my body during my throws for a powerful throwing position on the slick surface.

When the competition concluded, I was surprised to still be in second place. That meant I would receive a silver medal at the World Masters Indoor Championship for the shot put event, and I was again thrilled. Earlier in the day, my thoughts about being very sore from the previous day's javelin competition had almost caused me to not compete in the shot put event. Now, I had won the silver medal. What a shock!

The countries represented by the top three finishers were Poland, the United States and Estonia. The three of us were escorted down the hill to the main stadium for the award presentation. I had to stand on the podium in the second place spot, but was still very proud of my accomplishment. The Polish National Anthem was played after the medals were placed around our necks. Photos were taken, and we were soon on our way with broad smiles on our faces.

It had been a great competition for me. I would be wearing home both a gold and a silver medal around my neck for the United States. That made me a happy man, and I was glad to have traveled all the way to Daegu, South Korea for the 2017 World Masters Indoor Track and Field Championships.

Before I knew it, it was Wednesday. The previous night had been spent sleeping in spans of three hours. In-between I was wide awake and either read a book or watched the one English speaking channel on television. I did get nine hours of sleep, and was sure I would need that rest for the return flights and the long trip home.

After eating breakfast and checking out of my room, I caught a taxi to take me to the train station. I was carrying my large suitcase, a small backpack entirely stuffed, another large plastic bag with different items and souvenirs, plus my javelin in its 93" PVC carrying tube.

At the Dongdaegu train station, I found the main ticket

counter where they were holding my reservation. There was a young volunteer at the counter, a Korean girl, who spoke some broken English. She helped me through the process of getting my ticket for the train. Because I had two hours before my train would arrive, it allowed her time to take me around the station and explain the signs, so I would be able to catch the correct train. It was all very confusing to me.

Walking through the station, she pointed out where and when I should be positioned in order to catch my train. We even went downstairs to the boarding platforms to see how the individual trains were marked. At 12:50, I was to board train number 130, car number 5, and was assigned to seat 3A. Everything in the station was numbered, but many of the same numbers meant different things. My head was spinning with details, and the station was full of people. Because she took me on the tour, I felt confident I could work it out. She advised me to watch carefully as the time approached, so my train would not be missed. She said things could change quickly so be sure to watch the signs, which in general I couldn't read.

When we returned upstairs on the escalator, my hands were full, and I was holding the javelin tube in my left hand in a straight up position. She was in the process of giving me additional information, and my mind was totally focused on what she was saying in broken English while looking at her face. Suddenly, there was a loud noise that sounded like a gun shot. Everything happened so fast, I didn't realize immediately what had just occurred. The javelin tube had flexed in my left hand, and just as quickly, snapped backward and then forward. My heart started racing as I tried to figure out what was going on, but it was too late. By the time the noise was heard, it was all over.

Looking up, I noticed we had passed under a small overhang while going up the escalator. Because I had been holding the javelin for balance in an upright position, while resting it on the step, it had become wedged between the overhang and the step on the rising escalator. The tube holding my javelin had bent like a bow before it snapped loose and forward. Instantly, I knew my favorite metal javelin was damaged and my heart fell.

I sat down on a bench inside the train station and opened the end of the tube expecting the worst. My thinking was that the javelin had snapped into two pieces. Upon inspection, it was only bent. I made a quick mental decision to later send it to my friend, Ron Johnson in Oregon, who repaired javelins. In the past, he had helped me with repair work and would be able to straighten it before my next competition.

It had been a special javelin for me and had been used in big competitions for the past eight years. Something about its aero-dynamics seemed to allow it to travel a meter or so farther than the other two I owned. Surely, Ron could repair it and restore my confidence in its ability to travel straight and far through the air.

In thinking about that incident, its damage was a mental bum-mer for me, but I realized "shit happens." So many good things had happened so far on the trip that I wasn't going to worry about a repairable accident.

After a long wait of two hours and a nice Korean meal of pork, rice, steamed onions and melted cheese, I made my way down the escalator to the train platform. As I looked over to the spot where my javelin had earlier snagged the roof, I saw the surprising damage it had done to the ceiling. The escalator had trapped it as we rose, in such a way as to push it upward against the ceiling, bowing the tube and creating a lot of upward force. Part of the loud, gunshot-like noise I had heard was the complete roof, approximately twenty-five feet long, popping loose overhead as we passed under it. That was the reason the strong PVC tube did not break and only left the javelin bent and hopefully repairable. I thought about the cost that would be necessary to repair the ceiling and was glad to have not been arrested for the damage.

The train arrived right on time at 12:50, and I scrambled to board with my luggage. Car number 5 was written on the out-side. It was the right car, and the train was number 130. I could now relax. Seat 3A looked to be a comfortable seat. Shortly after placing everything on the small overhead rack, the train pulled out from the station. If I hadn't been standing right there when it pulled up, I would have never made it.

The train left the city and traveled at a speed of 60 to 70 miles per hour. For the next three hours, we passed through many little towns and the open countryside on the way to Seoul. We stopped five times briefly, to let off and pick up additional peo-ple. When the surrounding houses and buildings were not close to the train tracks, I could see a variety of gardens with people using hand tools digging rows of fresh dirt so they could later plant vegetables. It was still early spring, and they were working hard in order to get their seeds in the ground.

We reached our destination a little before 4:00 p.m., as the train pulled up to the edge of Incheon Airport. It was only a short five minute walk and up two flights of stairs to enter the airport. I followed the crowd and couldn't read any of the signs. Finally, I noticed an American Airlines logo and headed in that direction with my load of baggage that was getting heavier by the minute.

There was a smiling lady at the check-in counter, but she spoke very little English. She took my large suitcase and the javelin tube. I was told to pick them up after the long flight to the Dallas/Fort Worth Airport in Texas. That was where they would go through customs.

I went through security using my Global Entry Pass and boarded my plane where I would be seated for the next thirteen and a half hours. That wasn't bad because it had taken me more than fourteen and a half hours on my first flight six days earlier while flying west.

The next night was spent at a Comfort Inn five miles from the airport in Dallas. After eating supper at the motel restaurant, I went to my room to watch television, read a book for a short while and then go to sleep. The plan was to be in the lobby before 6:00 in the morning to catch the shuttle back to the airport for an 8:00 departure. Soon after landing in Charlotte for a two hour layover, another plane would fly me to Wilmington. Trent was scheduled to pick me up in the afternoon around 3:00. I was looking forward to that moment.

My trip had been tiring, but it was truly an adventure and a big success that I would remember for the rest of my life.

"The writing begins when you are finished.
Only then do you know
what you're trying to say."

Samuel Langhorne Clemens

Canada
June 2017

I began my trip to fish for king salmon in British Columbia, Canada with my younger son, Matt, on Wednesday, June 28th. He had recently turned thirty-three years old and was excited about getting to go on the fishing trip with me.

From Wilmington, I drove to Durham, N.C. and spent the night, so I could fly out the next morning on Southwest Airlines to Nashville. When I got to Nashville, Matt was waiting at the airport.

Shortly after I landed, we boarded the next Southwest flight going to Seattle. It had been seven months since I had seen him. We immediately began to have a good time as we sat next to each other on the plane. The trip was four and a half hours, and the time went fast as we talked continuously the whole way.

At the Seattle airport I picked up a rented, full-size car. We were quickly on our way north using Interstate 5 to Vancouver. That drive was 150 miles and took two and a half hours. On the way, we went through a check-point at the Canadian border. We finally arrived at the Pacific Gateway Hotel in Vancouver where we spent the night. It had been a long day since I had woken up at 3:30 a.m. in Durham. I realized I had been awake for twenty-two hours.

The following morning, we left our rental car at the hotel and took a shuttle to the airport. We boarded a small plane at the south terminal and flew north for an hour and thirty minutes. The south terminal was devoted mainly to fishing excursions going to the many lodges scattered throughout the area.

When we got off the plane in the afternoon at a small Indian fishing village named Bella Bella, the schedule had us quickly boarding a Kloehome water taxi. It took us directly to Joe's

Salmon Lodge. The boat ride took almost two hours. A brochure we had received earlier said it would be powered by Captain Bob and his crew. We ended up talking with the Captain along the way. He promised "stunning scenery" with possible whale and porpoise sightings. He also said the beauty around us had often been referred to as "God's Country."

Upon arriving that afternoon, we met Doug and Carl, co-owners of the lodge, along with their extensive staff of younger men and women. In the lodge lounge we were presented with what they called a "West Coast Feast" that came just in time, because we were very hungry. Their special mixed drink offered at the bar was named the "Uncle Doug." I decided I would enjoy a few of those over the next four days of fishing. The excitement was definitely beginning to build.

We were given a short orientation on how to operate our Boston Whaler boat, number eight, that Matt and I had been assigned to use. The fish master told us how to use the attached GPS and the radio which were mounted in each of the seventeen identical boats lined up side-by-side along the dock. Also, he told us how to rig the barb-free hooks into furnished herring bait. That explanation was given quickly, and I realized we were expected to learn mostly by trial and error.

No sooner than the group lesson had ended, it was time to get into the boats, so everyone could enjoy their first afternoon fishing for salmon. Once on board, we lined all of the boats up in single file and followed the fish master to our first suggested site twenty minutes away. We went through some rough seas. I had not been expecting the large swells and constant action of the ocean to be part of our trip. My previous Alaskan trip to catch salmon had been twenty years earlier. At that time, I had fished in a river that ran inland off the ocean. The water moved slowly with only a little current. That was what I had expected on this trip.

As a result of the ocean swells that first evening, Matt got a little seasick while trying to look down and focus on baiting his hook. I was glad he was the one baiting the fish hook instead of me, because I would have gotten extremely seasick if I hadn't continued to look out at the horizon while the boat bounced up and down. Motion sickness had always been a big problem for me, and I discovered it was for Matt also.

Even though the afternoon had started out warm and sunny, it wasn't long before the air turned cold with a light rain. We were wearing furnished rain gear, but the cold air seemed to go right through the rubber jacket and pants. Only one fish was caught out of our whole group of twenty-eight fishermen. We arrived back at the dock before dark at nearly ten o'clock.

There was a large supper waiting for us consisting of two kinds of pizza and a mixed salad. We visited with the other fishermen while eating and tried to remember everyone's name as we were introduced.

Soon it was time for bed. I was tired and fell asleep quickly around 11:00. Matt told me the next morning that he went to sleep forty minutes later.

I woke up at 5:00, and Matt got up around 9:00. He had been the drummer for a popular touring alternative rock band for the past eight years and had become used to getting up later in the morning. That was fine with me, because I viewed the trip as more about us being together than just catching fish.

The majority of the guests ate breakfast at a large table right outside our bedroom door. They made so much noise, I went ahead and got up shortly after 5:00. It was raining very hard that morning, but it didn't keep most of the fishermen from getting in their boats and heading out into the ocean shortly after daybreak.

Matt and I ate breakfast and got into our boat at 9:30. We traveled a short distance and fished near the rocky point of an island we had been told was a good spot and would be out of some of the strong turbulence of the open ocean. After two hours and no fish, we returned to the lodge for lunch.

Lunch was chicken and vegetable soup with hotdogs.

Definitely nothing special, but it filled us up. At 2:30, we started out again in the rain to try and catch our first king salmon. The first fish we caught were two ling cod fish that were quite ugly with spiked teeth and strongly patterned bodies. To me, they looked to be just "junk fish," so we released them. Next, Matt caught a medium sized flounder. I showed him how both eyes were on the same side of its head because it lay on the bottom all the time and looked up from a completely flat position. He had never seen one before.

At 4:30, Matt's rod finally dipped heavily, and we both knew it must be a large salmon. Before he could set the hook, the fish moved to my line and the drag on my reel started screaming from the line running off of it very fast. I lifted my rod tip and set the hook. I knew I needed to keep firm tension on the line due to the fact our hooks were barbless. Somehow, when that large salmon broke the surface for the first time, it shook my hook loose and was quickly gone. I would have liked to have put that fish in the boat, but it didn't happen.

By that time, we realized we needed to reel in our lines and go to the lodge for a five o'clock supper. Matt told me he was hungry again. After docking the boat and removing our rain gear and rubber boots, we enjoyed a thick steak, fried potatoes and salad. Matt ordered a double mixed drink, and I went to our room for a short break. I took my first shower and began to feel quite relaxed.

Matt returned to our room and told me there was a big decorated cake for dessert because it was Canada Day. I had no idea what that meant, but I left the room to enjoy some of the cake. I hoped the weather the next day would not be as cold and the constant rain would end. It had certainly been a messy first day. We had not put a single salmon in the boat.

Sunday morning, I was up at 5:30 to watch the majority of the other fishermen leave the lodge for their various fishing spots. They traveled in their assigned boats, each containing two men.

I waited for Matt to wake up and eat breakfast. We left the lodge later in the morning at 9:30.

Our starting spot for the day was a place three miles away named Baily's, marked by a large wooden triangle on the shore we could not miss seeing. Once we got there, an American bald eagle landed in the top of a nearby evergreen tree. It was beautiful and very large with a white head and white tail feathers. We fished aggressively up and down the shoreline beneath the eagle but received no bites. That was very frustrating for us, but we definitely knew it to be part of the fishing experience.

Before long, Matt sighted a large humpback whale not far away. It blew water high in the air before arching its back and rolling downward. We saw its large tail rise upward and then return with force to slap the surface. Before the morning trip concluded, the whale surfaced seven more times as we moved down the shoreline together.

We also saw two seals playing in the water not far from our boat. When we tried to move closer, they disappeared. At noon we went back to the lodge for a snack of red pepper soup and hotdogs. It was another OK meal, but we had been expecting a little more variety for lunch.

Around 2:30, we started out again and traveled to a place twenty-five minutes away named The Gap. It was near where the rough ocean pushed inland. That narrow opening, between two long islands, was rumored to be where many salmon had been caught in the past. We fished around the rocky shoreline, which was lined with large granite boulders. Otherwise, the land was covered by thick evergreen trees. There were other isolated islands with sharp outcrops close by, and we joked about naming one of them Hearn Corner. If we had caught a big fish there, the name might have stuck, but that didn't happen.

At The Gap, we hung our fishing lines numerous times in the thick kelp growing from the bottom of the ocean, and a couple of times we had to cut them loose. That was a problem because the rough sea swells made us seasick while retying the lines. We learned that each time our lines had to be retied, we had to move to calmer water behind an island to accomplish it. Then, we would return to the rougher water to start fishing again.

We tried and tried but only caught a four pound ling cod that day. At least we were happy to have a large fish in the boat. I believe if both of us had been willing to go to the other sites along with the other boats where the water was much rougher, we could have caught additional fish. Neither of us wanted to get seasick, so we didn't do that.

Five of the boats chose to go out into the open sea that was experiencing four foot swells. Their goal was to catch large, bottom feeding halibut at a depth of 300 feet. When I talked to those fishermen later in the day at the lodge, I found almost all of them had gotten very seasick. All the boats came back early with no halibut. Matt and I were glad we hadn't gone on that particular outing.

Supper was served at 6:00. We had only arrived back at the lodge thirty minutes earlier. There were some salmon being filleted at the cleaning station, but quantities were small considering how many people had been fishing all day. The weather had been better than the day before with only light scattered showers, but it had still been gloomy and overcast. Our faces were wind burned from the wind and the cold and not from the sun.

We enjoyed grilled ribs, chicken, salad and a nice sweet dessert before sitting around and talking in small groups with the other guests. Later, I went out to our small boat and spent an hour retying the lines on all three rods in preparation for the next day of fishing.

Because our luck had been so bad, Matt told me he wanted to get up earlier the following day for an all-out attempt to catch some salmon. So far, we had only one large salmon temporarily on the line before it slipped off the hook. While fishing with no barb, the hook had been easily thrown from the fish's mouth.

Before going to bed, I thought about the fun we were having. It had been enjoyable to joke and talk with Matt about all kinds of things. We went to sleep knowing that each of us was looking forward to our next day of fishing together when we might catch a big one.

On Monday morning I was recharged and excited about the new day. I had been up since 4:30 when the rest of the group first started making noise at the breakfast table. The night before, I had fallen asleep at 11:00 and had ended up with a good night's rest. Matt had gone to bed later, but I was hoping he would be up in an hour or so feeling refreshed and ready to go.

Monday would be our last complete day to fish. For us, so far, the results had been grim. We hoped we would get lucky and put a couple of nice salmon in the boat. My original plan had been for Matt to take home a frozen, fifty pound box of filleted salmon that we would catch together. I had planned to do the same. We had both purchased small freezers for our homes in which to store the fillets after we got back.

The weather cleared by mid-morning, but it was still cold and overcast. Both Matt and I had been having a great time together, so the extra effort and pressure to catch a lot of fish didn't really matter. We knew we could always go to the store when we got home and buy a few nice salmon filets. I thought that was the best way to start thinking, because we weren't catching anything of importance.

At 9:00, we started the boat motor and moved toward a recommended spot a few miles away. The clouds and rain were with us, but by the time we started fishing the skies became sunny. It was a dramatic change, and we hadn't even brought our brimmed hats that morning. As a result, we both got bad sunburns on our faces.

Within fifteen minutes, Matt caught his first king salmon, which in British Columbia was referred to as a spring salmon. That fish weighed in at fifteen pounds. We were both very happy about the catch.

It wasn't twenty minutes later that my rod dipped heavily,

and the reel started feeding off line. As I set the hook, I instantly knew I had a big one. It jumped out of the water, so I plainly saw its impressive size. In playing the fish around the water, with tension on the line, I was afraid it might slip off before we could get it into the net. When it was finally tired enough to get close to the boat, Matt tried to get it in our large, three foot wide, heavy nylon net. The salmon was so big and powerful, it instantly stuck its nose through one of the small mesh holes in the net. With a quick thrust of its tail, the fish pushed a large hole in the lowest part of the strong net and swam, with the fishing line, completely through the opening that had been created. It then swam fast and dove deep while running away from us.

I instantly knew trying to land the fish with the line through the net would be a big problem as soon as it happened. Somehow, I kept the line tight and directed Matt to position the frame of the net in line with my rod as I tried to fight the fish through the opening in the net. Matt had to move back and forth in the boat with the net to keep up with the fish that moved from one direc- tion to the other.

While I doubted we would ever get the fish in the boat, I noticed another dilemma. The large eight ounce lead weight attached to the line had become hung in the cording of the nylon net. That compounded our problem. I told Matt to move the net up and down as the fish pulled outward, and to move it back and forth as the fish raced from left to right.

Finally, the salmon looked to be tiring. Our only hope was to get it quickly into the net and twist the metal frame sideways before the fish slipped through the hole again. Matt netted the fish, twisted the net just right, and we both lifted it into the boat. To get the hook out, I had to club the large, aggressive fish over the head above the eyes with a small bat, and then it settled down.

We looked in amazement as the fish lay on the floor of the boat and then gave each other a high five in celebration. We had done the impossible. When the king salmon was weighed at the dock, it tipped the scales at 32 pounds. We later learned that in that part of the country, any king salmon over thirty pounds was considered very large and earned a special award. The captain later gave us a nice enameled pin making us members of the Tyee Club, as a result of catching that salmon. It was the second largest salmon caught by anyone on our four day fishing trip. That included twenty-eight of us fishermen who fished hard each day. The owner of the lodge, Doug, took a nice photo of us with the fish as it was weighed at the dock and posted it on his Facebook page as advertisement for Joe's Salmon Lodge.

As it turned out, that was not the only excitement of the day. Forty-five minutes later, I hooked another large salmon, and when setting the hook while using a ten foot long flexible rod, the rod snapped in half. The fish had pulled downward with such resistance, at the same time I had snatched upward with the rod, the rod exploded in the middle. When that happened, the short end of the rod with the reel attached hit me squarely in the face with great force. The sensation was like getting hit with a baseball bat, and I was temporarily stunned. As I staggered backward and assessed how badly I had been injured, I noticed the fish was still hooked and running out line off my reel. There I was, holding the reel and a short part of the rod that was now only three feet long instead of ten feet. The trick was to find a way to keep the line tight so the barbless hook would not come out of its mouth.

After I played the fish around for a short time, Matt was able to get the net under it. It was smaller than the earlier one at only thirteen pounds but still a very nice king salmon. By that time, we knew we would be going back to the dock with some impressive fish.

There was one other exciting catch that afternoon, with Matt hooking another salmon. When he set the hook, his rod also broke in half, and he found himself fighting the salmon with only a four foot rod that had no flex. It was later landed by using patience, mixed with a little luck. We were the only fishermen who broke two rods, and I believe it had to do with how forceful we were trying to set the hook. We learned that the long, flexible rods would not take much stress. We decided to let the fish hook themselves while pulling downward, instead of jerking so hard.

As we drove the boat back to the lodge through the rolling open ocean, I looked over and Matt was smiling. We had together beaten the odds and landed a few good fish that should have never been caught.

On Tuesday morning, we were allowed two more hours of fishing before leaving for home. We hoped to land at least one more big salmon. That happened within thirty minutes as we netted a fourteen pounder. The fish was cleaned quickly when we arrived back at the dock and put in the freezer. Its additional weight filled out the total of what we wanted to take home. As a result of our luck on the last couple of days, we ended our fishing trip with 100 pounds of fillets that we split into two large boxes. Matt took half of the frozen salmon to Nashville, and I took the other half home to Wilmington.

In the afternoon that final day, we rode the river taxi south to the same small Indian fishing village, Bella Bella, which we had traveled through on the day of our arrival. From there, we were scheduled to board another medium-sized prop plane, with our boxed and frozen fish, that would take us to Vancouver.

It turned out, just a short while after arriving at the small airport, there was more excitement to come. The prop plane was waiting for us and had originally been scheduled to take off at 4:00. By 5:00, everyone began to ask questions about the holdup, because we had not yet been allowed to board. We discovered from Doug that the airport personnel had determined we were carrying too much weight to be able to take off. There were 28 fishermen, plus Doug and his wife, along with the many boxes of frozen fish. The airport officials were seriously afraid the small plane would not lift off the ground. In order to lower the weight, Doug started asking people to stay behind and take a later plane. No one wanted to do that, so we all became trapped in a stalemate.

Finally, some of the guys agreed to leave behind their frozen salmon, if it could be shipped to them the following day. That meant removing some of the boxes already loaded on the plane. Even after doing that, we calculated we still had five hundred pounds to go to be able to take off safely. Doug and his wife finally agreed to stay overnight with their two boxes of frozen fish, so the plane would be allowed to leave. He was a big man and weighed 275 pounds and his wife was about 120 pounds. Their two boxes of fish totaled one hundred pounds. That was the remaining weight we needed off the plane before the pilot said, "We might be able to get off the ground."

Everyone else was allowed to board the plane, but we were all very concerned. We were told the wind had to be blowing toward the front of the plane to get it off the ground. The plane taxied to the extreme end of the small runway as we waited for a change in wind direction. There was much worry and conversation throughout the plane as we looked at each other. Everyone was wondering whether we would end up in the trees at the end of the runway or get into the air successfully.

Suddenly, the pilot announced he was going to attempt to lift the overloaded plane off the ground during a quick change of wind direction. He gunned the engines, and down the runway we raced. Building speed, I looked out the small window to see the scenery moving quickly by us.

I knew everyone was thrilled as the plane finally left the ground at the end of the runway and soared slightly over the treetops. As we climbed to 25,000 feet, there were many sighs of relief.

The rest of the trip home was somewhat uneventful. We reversed everything we had gone through to arrive just a few days earlier.

Matt and I had a great time together. We caught some nice salmon and created long-lasting memories. We were certain we would learn to cook salmon in a variety of ways using what we had caught on the trip.

*My philosophy of life is that if we make up
our minds what we are going
to make of our lives, then work hard
toward that goal,
we never lose—
somehow we win out.*

Ronald Reagan

Bonaire
January 2018

One of my favorite places to visit is the little island of Bonaire. It is located approximately twenty miles off the northeastern shore of Venezuela in South America. There are three small isolated islands in that area and they are collectively referred to as the ABC islands. That would be Aruba, Bonaire and Curacao.

Bonaire is only twenty miles long, and there are not many people who live there permanently. When we first visited the island about ten years ago, I was told there were around thirteen thousand residents. On our most recent trip, I was told that number was now closer to eighteen thousand. The people speak English and are very friendly to tourists. Those two things combine to make it a wonderful place to visit. We've been there on short vacations as many as seven times and hope to go back next year.

I like to go there mainly to snorkel and enjoy the island's reef life. The water on the leeward side is always calm and extremely clear. Visibility is normally at least one hundred feet. I can usually read wording on other snorkeler's or diver's shirts from that distance while I am under water.

There has been a big push by the islanders to keep the reefs and water around Bonaire as pristine as possible. They realize the importance of conservation in retaining a beautiful and unusual place for themselves and for tourists. The purchase of a small plastic tag is required to use the waters around the island. The tag only costs ten dollars if you plan to snorkel or twenty-five dollars if you want to scuba dive. It is worn on the side of the face mask attached by a plastic band. That money is used to keep the beaches clean. It also goes toward maintaining a small nature park on the northwestern corner of the island. To drive into that park, you are required to have a four wheel drive vehicle because many of the roads have no pavement. After a short rain, the mud on the roads can make it difficult to maneuver with a normal car. There are two nice snorkeling beaches in the western edge of the park, but the snorkeling around the entire shoreline of the island is so nice it is not necessary to go there to enjoy the water.

Upon entering the water from a broken coral covered beach, the reef can be reached within thirty feet. Usually there will be an opening through which I can pass to get on the back side of the reef, and water there may be from six to twelve feet deep. Instantly, there will be visible a variety of fish swimming either alone or in small groups. It is not uncommon to see a school of one hundred purple tangs within minutes of entering the water. There will also be smaller groups of fish like wrasses, angelfish or a variety of parrotfish passing over the individual coral heads.

I like to rent a vehicle, carry my snorkel gear and stop randomly along the shoreline at any spot that looks inviting. Since I normally snorkel alone, I wear a small inflatable vest that serves as a life jacket. I keep a small amount of air in the vest, and it keeps me on the surface comfortably. I can lean forward and enjoy the warm, clear, tropical water of Bonaire while enjoying the reef life below.

Along the shore and just past the breaker reefs, I can slowly drift snorkel without the use of artificial fins on my feet. Over fifteen years ago, I discontinued wearing fins and have never gotten myself into a problem with strong currents. Whenever I approach an area where the water current is beginning to pick up speed, I just back off to where I know I can swim with my arms to a safer place. I normally wear rubber booties to protect my feet around the coral.

A normal day of snorkeling in Bonaire for me would include about two to three hours in the water. After I work myself through the reef only a short distance from shore, I begin to swim slowly parallel to the beach in one direction. Along the way, I notice creatures like octopuses, flounders, eels and occasionally a Caribbean lobster coming out from a hole in the white sand or a group of rocks below. These are all fun to see. Usually when I spot one of them, I will stay on the surface and remain quite still. Octopuses especially are very interesting to me. It is obvious that they possess a high level of intelligence by the way they move. With their small eyes peering up at me, they glide over the bottom in search of another hiding place or look for a small fish or creature to eat. Their color and texture change quickly as they pass over different objects on the bottom. They can go from dark and rough to white and smooth in a matter of seconds. It's an amazing transformation to observe.

Flounders are similar to the octopuses in the way they can change color. At first, a blue spotted white flounder will remain completely still, slightly buried in the sand. Then in just a second, it will get darker and glide effortlessly across the bottom to a new location. They are hard to spot originally but always fun to watch. Both eyes are on the same side of their head. By hovering over them on the surface, it is easy to see their eyes move around while checking out the environment. I know they are watching me, and if I get too close, they are quick to move to deeper water.

The eels have different colors with varying body patterns. They look a lot like snakes and rarely lift their bodies above the sand. Their eyes are always searching for small openings in the reef or a large rock to slither under. I try to never get too close to the eels, especially the moray eels, because they do have the ability to bite if irritated. The moray eels can reach up to four feet in length with a width of ten inches, including their upper fins. They are very intimidating because of the white spiked teeth easily seen in their green jaws. I've found if I don't bother them, they don't bother me. A few years ago, a large one slowly swam past me within five feet while checking me out. After it passed, it soon entered a hole in a nearby group of rocks. The large eels are especially fun to see.

The Caribbean lobster is harder to locate and not seen very often. It is a beautiful creature with colors of rust, brown, black and off-white hues mixed in a variety of patterns on its body. It doesn't have claws like the Maine lobster, but it does have two very long feelers extending from its head. They are spiked, and those spikes will stick in your hand if you grab the lobster without using a glove. Once grabbed, it will twist and jerk violently. The best way to catch one is to use a large net with a long handle. That way you can get the net around it before it scurries into a hole, and you don't get stuck by the spikes. They are good to eat but protected in some areas.

Some of the larger fish seen in quantities around Bonaire are the parrotfish. There are many different species living close to the shore. They are all very colorful and fun to observe. Usually they will allow a snorkeler to get within five feet before moving away slowly. Some, like the emerald green rainbow parrotfish, can reach a length of four feet. The upper dorsal fin and tail is covered with a brilliant rust color which creates a strong contrast with its iridescent green body. They are seen feeding on algae in the shallow water between the reef's top layer and the surface of the water. With the incoming waves and the gentle ocean surge, it is hard to image them wanting to feed in that spot. I think it may have to do with the fact they feel protected in that tight area.

Another species of beautiful parrotfish seen frequently is the stoplight parrotfish. The females look distinctly different from the males. They are covered with spots of color on their scales that resemble a checkerboard. Patterns of white, dark gray and red alternate and cover their sides. Their bellies are a red-orange color. Otherwise, they are a cream color with lines of gray and black. I'm told the females and males look alike until the males begin to reach maturity. At that time the males change considerably. They take on a rainbow of color and lose all of their checkerboard patterning. The adult male is referred to as a terminal phase, stoplight parrotfish. It is covered with beautiful blue, green, yellow, orange, pink, purple and cream colors.

They are always enjoyable to see, and I try to observe them closely as they use their front teeth to chew on the coral. I have been told that all the sand on the beaches around the world was created by parrotfish chewing on coral. They filter the part they eat for nutrients and poop out the crushed white sand that was originally the surface of a coral head. The crushed sand particles eventually wash to the shore to become our beaches.

There are also queen parrotfish, princess parrotfish, and blue parrotfish. All are beautiful variations that continually chew on the coral. While snorkeling, I can hear them grinding their upper and lower buck teeth on the coral and later see them pooping out the sand.

Along the leeward side of the island where the water is mostly calm, I normally use my rental car to take me to marked spots that have easy access to the ocean. Most of them are marked by yellow painted rocks with identifying names roughly written in black paint. There are maybe thirty of those spots marked by the famous yellow rocks. A few of the popular sites for beginning snorkelers are Andrea I and Andrea II. Another popular dive site marked by one of the stones is named 1,000 steps. There, to get to the beach from a small area where the cars are parked, you have to descend down about ninety stone steps formed into a cliff face. The way it got the name has to do with the fact that if you carry a scuba tank, flippers, and other gear to the beach below, it seems like you went down 1,000 steps. Later, when you return to your car, it seems like an additional 1,000 steps up the cliff.

Over the years on Bonaire, we have stayed at a place named Captain Don's Habitat. It's a strange name, but a relaxing place with a very nice restaurant. It is located near the middle of the island at the edge of the water. It has a row of rental houses positioned right by the beach. You can leave one of the houses and be snorkeling in less than a minute. Captain Don's has dive boats available and those boats go out at least twice a day with many eager divers on board. The resort has a dive shop full of everything needed and offers air to fill your rental tanks.

Next door is another popular dive resort named Buddy Dive. We have never stayed there, but it is similar to Captain Don's with its small fleet of dive boats and helpful employees. We prefer Captain Don's because the rental houses are nicer and the restaurant is outstanding. At night, while eating by the edge of a slight rock drop-off, a group of tarpon can be seen swimming together under the spotlights. During the day when I swam with them, some were as long as six feet.

There are large broken coral pieces washed up everywhere on the beaches, so the shoreline in most places is not your normal white sandy beach. There are little lizards and larger iguanas roaming those areas looking for food. If you feed them, they will be with you for the day. Trent can verify that while lying on the ground sunbathing, it would not be uncommon for one of them to creep up quietly and nip your toe. I've learned they are only looking for food and have been fed in the past by tourists. They will startle you but not hurt you.

One night, I joined a group of five individuals from Buddy Dive who wanted to go snorkeling at the pier downtown around 10:00. I had snorkeled and scuba dived in a freshwater lake after dark but never in the ocean. I figured it would be exciting and had no idea what I might see.

We had to first get permission from the dock master to be in that area after dark because it was where the cruise ships docked during the day. That night there were no cruise ships, so we were allowed access. I had a special flashlight that would shine through the water for up to thirty feet. Each of us carried one. If I had been alone, I would have been concerned, but since I was snorkeling with others, I knew I would be OK. The water was twenty five feet deep and very clear. We swam under the dock and observed all kinds of creatures and fish living either on or around the pilings of the dock. I saw a lobster clinging to one of the circular pilings along with a variety of sponges, crabs and colorful fish. They were moving around in groups with no concern about us being in the water with the bright lights. After a couple of hours, we got out of the water and talked about what we had seen. I was glad I had taken the time to go on that outing.

Off shore and only a half mile away, there is a small uninhabited island named Klein Bonaire. It is one of the reasons Bonaire is such a special place. The snorkeling around that island and its reef is fantastic. The trip starts when a river taxi stops at a hotel dock and picks up around thirty people. For a small fee, the taxi takes them to the island and drops them off. It travels there and back every two hours. It only takes fifteen minutes to get everyone to the white sand beaches on the east side of the island. Many people only want to lie in the sun on the sand. For me, I like the river taxi to drop me off a mile up current and up wind, so I can drift snorkel down the entire outer edge of the island. Once in the water, the depth quickly changes from sixty feet deep to around ten feet deep as I get near the reef. I am free to take as much time as I want to drift down the entire side of the island with the gentle breeze and light current.

The best time to do the drift snorkel is when the sun is shining brightly. That is true most of the time when snorkeling. When the sun is out, everything is very visible in the water. The colors of the fish and coral are beautiful. When first dropped off, it is normal to see a few green sea turtles swimming around large tube sponges and other tall sponges extending off the bottom in clusters. The bottom has a gentle slope toward the reef covered by white sand, so that everything is easily seen. There is always a variety of fish to see swimming in the area.

There are file fish with varying colors of rust, black, yellow and white. They are very friendly and will sometimes come right up to my face mask. That is also true of the French angelfish. Many of them are fully adult and almost fifteen inches long. It seems as if every time I'm there, there are two of them following me down the reef, much to my enjoyment. Many small fish are always seen swimming around the coral heads, and I try to stop and hover over them to watch. Sometimes I see cleaner fish working at what is called a cleaner station. The little slender fish, that would normally be quickly eaten, are allowed to peck parasites off the sides and gills of the larger fish. The bigger fish will sometimes just lie over on their sides as the cleaner fish move over their bodies. It is something special to observe.

A few years ago, I observed a lionfish along the reef at Klein Bonaire. It was fully adult and fifteen inches in length with long flowing fins. The lionfish used to be unusual in the area and not normally found in waters other than around the Philippines in the Indo-Pacific Ocean on the other side of the earth. It arrived on the east coast of the United States through the aquarium trade. People imported them, kept them in saltwater aquariums, and eventually released them into the ocean. The fish began to multiply and travel with the warm currents of the Gulf Stream.

The lionfish are not wanted in Bonaire, or in any other place, but in the last thirty years they have shown up everywhere in warm water. They have no natural predators. The problem is they eat the small baby groupers, snappers and others living around the coral heads. They can be found in the waters from Maine to Florida, through the Gulf of Mexico and down as far as the northern edge of South America.

I was told at the dive shop in Bonaire to report any lionfish I saw, so divers could be sent out to capture it. They don't want them to take over the area. After my sighting, I reported it, and I'm sure it was later captured. I believe the people of Bonaire are fighting a losing battle with the lionfish because those predator fish lay thousands of eggs each year. Once the eggs hatch and the fish mature, they scatter and eat many of the other species of baby fish.

There are many nice restaurants in Bonaire along the beach or just a few miles away in the downtown area. We have eaten at many of them. Most offer specialties involving all types of local fish. The last time we were there, we again ate at a very nice place named It Rains Fishes. It is located downtown by the water, overlooking many moored fishing boats, with an excellent view of the sunset. We arrived just ten minutes before the sun went down, and afterwards the display of reddish color in the clouds lasted for at least fifteen minutes. It was a great evening.

There are other outstanding restaurants, including the one I mentioned earlier at Captain Don's Habitat. Under the open night sky and stars, the food is always tasty. Their wood fired pizza is delicious. If you want to get fast food, there is a Kentucky Fried Chicken restaurant that we visit occasionally.

Downtown Bonaire has a small group of buildings lining one main street. It's near where the cruise ships come in and that traffic is probably what keeps those stores open and thriving. They offer all of the standard tourists' items including jewelry, clothing and souvenirs. At least once on every trip, I go there to wander through the shops to see if anything new is being featured. I usually eat lunch at one of the restaurants there. Those places serve some of the local beer that I enjoy.

Overall, Bonaire is a great place. It has impressed me with its simplicity every time I've been there. It's a place to just kick back and relax. At the moment, we are scheduled to again visit Bonaire next January with some friends. I can hardly wait for that trip.

A man who enjoys true success
is a man who controls
his own time, freedom, attitude
and destiny, while staying aware
of the needs of others around him.

Ed Hearn

About the Author

Edward Joseph Hearn was born in Nashville, Tennessee on June 26, 1949 and lived there for his first fifty years. He attended Tennessee Preparatory School from the fifth grade until graduation in 1967. Afterwards, he graduated from Tennessee Technological University with a major in Business Management. He later worked at a manufacturing/printing business in Nashville for thirty years where he served as an outside salesperson and part-owner.

He has two sons, John Edward and Matthew Robert, and two grandchildren, John Owen and Isabella Marie. The decision to retire came for Ed two decades ago, and since then he has lived as part of the Landfall community in Wilmington, North Carolina near the beaches of the Atlantic Ocean. Before retirement, he lived at the edge of a large, freshwater lake in middle Tennessee, and after retirement he enjoyed a second home located on a lake near Charlotte, North Carolina.

Ed enjoys playing golf and tennis, boating, fishing, traveling, writing, creating highly-detailed, fine-art sculptures made of wood and bronze, producing acrylic paintings and participating in masters track and field competitions throughout the United States and around the world.

He has written both entertaining and thoughtful short stories for many years in an effort to eventually share them in published books. His intentions were to document his colorful life and varied experiences through his memories for both his extended family and other interested individuals.

While traveling on some of his major trips to other countries, he kept detailed journals and later converted them into this book.